W9-BWR-060

A HISTORICAL READER

The Challenge of
Terrorism

nextext

Printed in the United States of America

ISBN 0-618-23616-3

1 2 3 4 5 6 7 — QKT — 08 07 06 05 04 03 02

Table of Contents

Throughout the reader, vocabulary words appear in boldface type and are footnoted. Specialized or technical words and phrases appear in lightface type and are footnoted.

Introduction

Episodes of Terrorism, 1963–1995

Terrorists act from a variety of motives, including religion, ethnicity, and politics. They also use a variety of methods to achieve their goals. These methods include kidnapping, murder, hijacking, bombing, and attacks with chemical or biological weapons. This sampling of episodes of terrorism from the later 20th century gives an introduction to the range of terrorists' motives and methods.

Birmingham, Alabama, September 15, 1963

The response of a small group of Southern racists to the Civil Rights Movement of the 1950s and 1960s was a terror campaign of kidnappings, murder, and bombings. The worst episode was the bombing of the 16th Street Baptist Church in Birmingham, Alabama.

Algiers, Algeria, July 22, 1968

After Israel won the Six Day War in 1967, some Palestinians turned to terrorism as their weapon against Israel. The Popular Front for the Liberation of Palestine hijacked an Israeli El Al flight from Rome to Tel Aviv, Israel. The flight was diverted to Algeria, where the terrorists held the Israeli passengers hostage until August 31. Airline hijackings and bombings became the principal methods of Palestinian terrorism over the next decade and a half.

Belfast, Northern Ireland, July 21, 1972

The Irish Republican Army is dedicated to the cause of forcing the British to abandon Northern Ireland. In 1969, this decades-old conflict entered its most violent phase when the IRA began a terrorist campaign of bombings, sniper attacks, and kidnappings in Northern Ireland and England. On "Bloody Friday," July 21, 1972, IRA attacks in Belfast, Northern Ireland, killed 9 people.

Munich, West Germany, September 5, 1972

During the Summer Olympic Games, heavily armed Arab terrorists attacked the Israeli team in the Olympic Village. They killed two Israeli athletes and took nine others hostage, demanding the release of 200 Palestinian prisoners in Israel. All nine hostages, five terrorists, and a West German policeman were killed that night in a failed rescue attempt.

Cologne, West Germany, September 5, 1977

During the 1970s, some communist groups in Europe began to use terrorism. They hoped to bring about revolution by attacking the governments, the military, and corporations. On September 5, 1977, members of the Red Army Faction (better known as the Baader-Meinhof Gang) kidnapped and later murdered Hanns-Martin Schleyer, a West German businessman. The Baader-Meinhof Gang had been conducting a campaign of bombings and kidnappings in West Germany.

Rome, Italy, March 16, 1978

Aldo Moro, who had been the leader of the Italian government five times, was kidnapped on his way to parliament by the Red Brigades. The Red Brigades was a communist terrorist group dedicated to bringing down society and beginning a revolution. They demanded the release of 13 of their comrades on trial for previous acts of terrorism. Moro was held for 54 days and then murdered.

Beirut, Lebanon, January 20, 1987

In the 1980s, radical Islamic guerrillas in Lebanon began kidnapping Westerners in Beirut. The terrorists held them hostage in an attempt to gain the release of jailed comrades and to draw attention to their cause. Englishman Terry Waite was in Lebanon trying to gain the release of American hostages when he himself was taken captive.

Lockerbie, Scotland, December 21, 1988

Pan Am flight 103 blew up somewhere over Lockerbie 38 minutes after taking off from London en route to New York. A bomb set by Libyan intelligence officers killed all 243 passengers and 16 crew members aboard the plane and 11 townspeople on the ground. Throughout the 1970s and 1980s, the Libyans had supported pro-Palestinian and anti-American terrorism.

Sriperumbudur, India, May 21, 1991

Rajiv Gandhi, a former prime minister of India, was killed by a Tamil Tiger suicide bomber at a campaign rally. The Liberation Tigers of Tamil Eelam are fighting for a Tamil national homeland in Sri Lanka, an island nation off the southeast coast of India. They were taking revenge against Gandhi for sending Indian soldiers to help the Sri Lankan government fight the Tigers.

New York City, February 26, 1993

A truck bomb exploded in a parking garage below the World Trade Center. The blast killed six people and injured more than a thousand others. The FBI quickly arrested four radical Muslims, who were convicted in 1994.

Tokyo, Japan, March 20, 1995

Members of the Aum Shinrikyo ("Supreme Truth") cult released Sarin nerve gas in a crowded Tokyo subway station, killing 12 people and injuring more than 5,500 others. The Aum Shinrikyo cult believes the world is soon to end.

Oklahoma City, Oklahoma, April 19, 1995

At 9:02 A.M., a powerful truck bomb exploded in front of the Alfred P. Murrah Federal Building and killed 168 people. At first, investigators believed international terrorists had caused the explosion. Later, it was proved that Timothy McVeigh, a former U.S. soldier, had set off the bomb. McVeigh believed that the U.S. government was the enemy of freedom and that any government site was a legitimate target in his "war" against it.

The coroner's office identified the four girls killed at the church as (from left) Denise McNair, 11; Carole Robertson, 14; Addie Mae Collins, 10; and Cynthia Wesley, 14.

Six Dead After Church Bombing

Birmingham, Sept. 15 (UPI)–A bomb hurled from a passing car blasted a crowded Negro church today, killing four girls in their Sunday school classes and triggering outbreaks of violence that left two more persons dead in the streets.

Dozens of survivors, their faces dripping blood from the glass that flew out of the church's stained glass windows, staggered around the building in a cloud of white dust raised by the explosion. The blast crushed two nearby cars like toys and blew out windows blocks away.

▲

The size of the crater produced by the bomb convinced a Birmingham police inspector that as many as 15 sticks of dynamite must have been used.

The only stained glass window in the church that remained in its frame shows Christ leading a group of little children. The face of Christ was blown out. ▶

An Israeli Airliner Hijacked to Algeria

Tel Aviv, Tuesday, July 22 (Reuters)—An Israeli airliner flying from Rome to Lydda with 10 crew members and 38 passengers was hijacked and diverted to Algeria today.

Sources at the Lydda airport said that the El Al Israel Airlines plane landed safely in Algeria at 2:35 A.M., about two and a half hours after it left Rome.

The sources said that the airline and the Israeli Government had started action to get the plane passengers and crew released immediately.

▲

12 of the Israeli passengers and crew on board were held hostage for five weeks. This was the first (and last) successful hijacking of an Israeli airliner.

Background Immediately after the hijacking, an Arab group, the Popular Front for the Liberation of Palestine, claimed responsibility. In Tel Aviv, the Israeli government condemned the act as "airborne piracy."

Belfast Bombings Kill at Least 13 and Wound 130

Belfast, Northern Ireland, Saturday, July 22 (The New York Times)—Belfast was struck yesterday by a coordinated bombing attack in which at least 13 people were killed and 130 were wounded.

Guerrillas of the outlawed Irish Republican Army set off 22 blasts in the afternoon within about 80 minutes, creating scenes of terror at shopping centers, bus and railroad stations, hotels, truck depots, a bank, a newspaper office and a bridge.

More than 100 persons injured in the bombings were hospitalized last night, according to a police spokesman. He said that children accounted for about a quarter of the casualties.

Since the late 1960s, militant Catholics and Protestants in Northern Ireland have both engaged in terrorism.

The Irish Republican Army carried out terrorist campaigns in England as well, including this 1973 bombing attack in London's Whitehall district, where many government offices are located.

▼

9 Israelis on Olympic Team Killed with 4 Arab Captors as Police Fight Band that Disrupted Munich Games

Munich, West Germany, Wednesday, Sept. 6 (The New York Times)—Eleven members of Israel's Olympic team and four Arab terrorists were killed yesterday in a 23-hour drama that began with an invasion of the Olympic Village by the Arabs. It ended in a shootout at a military airport some 15 miles away as the Arabs were preparing to fly to Cairo with their Israeli hostages.

The bloodshed brought the suspension of the Olympic Games, and there was doubt if they would be resumed.

Background The Arab terrorists, known as the Black September Group, occupied the building where the Israeli athletes were staying, killing two and taking nine others hostage.

A convoy of West German riot police entered the Olympic Village in an unsuccessful attempt to rescue the hostages.

The hostages were killed in an airport shootout between their Arab captors and West German police and soldiers. This helicopter was destroyed by a hand grenade set off by one of the terrorists.

German Kidnapped; 4 Guards Are Slain

Cologne, West Germany, Sept. 5 (Reuters)—Gunmen kidnapped one of West Germany's leading industrialists and killed four of his bodyguards today in an attack on his automobile during the evening rush hour.

The police speculated that the killers might have been left-wing urban guerrillas, but there was no immediate indication of who they were.

Background 10–15 gunmen in a small yellow bus attacked the industrialist's motorcade at a crossroads in the evening rush hour, spraying it with machine-gun fire. Two police escorts, a security agent, and a driver died instantly.

◀ The kidnapped industrialist was 62-year-old Dr. Hanns-Martin Schleyer, the president of the West German Confederation of Employers' Association and president of the Federation of West German Industries. This picture was released by his captives to prove that he was alive. He was later murdered.

The terrorists sought in the kidnapping and murder of Hanns-Martin Schleyer were the Red Army Faction, better known as the Baader-Meinhof Gang. ▼

Background Moro was held in captivity for 54 days before he was murdered. His body was found in a van parked on a street in Rome.

The Red Brigades (Italian, "Brigate Rosse") later issued this "death sentence" for Moro. ▶

Ex-Premier Is Discovered in Car on Downtown Street 54 Days After Abduction

Rome, May 9 (The New York Times)—The bullet-riddled body of former Prime Minister Aldo Moro was abandoned by his kidnappers today in a parked car in the historic center of Rome, a short distance from the headquarters of both the Communist and Christian Democratic parties, whose alliance the terrorist Red Brigades are fighting to destroy.

The discovery of the body behind the back seat of a burgundy red French Renault R-4 came 54 days after Mr. Moro, who was expected to be the next president of Italy, was abducted in a hail of gunfire in a street near his suburban home by urban guerrillas belonging to the Red Brigades.

▲ Five of Aldo Moro's bodyguards were killed when Red Brigade terrorists kidnapped him on March 16, 1978.

Envoy Detained by Hezbollah Forces, Diplomatic Sources Say

Beirut, Lebanon, January 31, 1987 (The Los Angeles Times)—
Anglican Church envoy Terry Waite is being detained by
fundamentalist Hezbollah forces in Lebanon in a political
tug-of-war between the militant Shia Muslim group,
which has close ties to Iran, and Druze leader Walid
Jumblatt, diplomatic sources said Friday.

Waite, who was working for the release of reporter
Terry A. Anderson and educator Thomas M. Sutherland,
has not been seen for 11 days.

Background In the early 1980s, Waite had successfully negotiated the release of several hostages from Iran. He later gained the release of British hostages held in Libya.

The terrorists who kidnapped Waite kept him a prisoner for nearly five years. He is shown here in Damascus on the day of his release, November 18, 1991. The first four years of his captivity were spent in solitary confinement.

▼

Town's Hall Used as Clinic, Then Morgue

Lockerbie, Scotland, Dec. 21 (AP)–Soon after the Pan Am Boeing 747 plowed into Lockerbie this evening, its council hall became a makeshift clinic. Within hours, it was a morgue.

Nobody knows how many of the 2,500 villagers have lost their lives, but many houses were flattened, and others caught fire and were gutted.

Mayor Frank Park stood in the street, dazed and in tears, too distraught to talk. Pleasant village lanes were littered with debris, masonry, ripped up fences, and shrubbery.

Royal Air Force rescue authorities say two rows of houses were demolished and no survivors have been found in the wreckage.

▲
Soldiers search the crater left by the wreckage of the downed Pan Am flight.

Background Pan Am flight 103 was destroyed by a terrorist bomb, killing all 259 passengers and crew. Here, a policeman walks beside the wreckage of the cockpit.

Gandhi Is Murdered in Bombing

Sriperumbudur, India, May 22 (Houston Chronicle)—Former Prime Minister Rajiv Gandhi, the son and grandson of prime ministers, was assassinated by a bomb hidden in a flower pot Tuesday at an election rally.

There was no immediate claim of responsibility for the attack in Sriperumbudur, a village 25 miles southwest of Madras in the state of Tamil Nadu.

The assassination raised fears of increased bloodshed in India after the most violent election campaign in the country's 44 years of independence.

When word of the assassination spread, gangs of young men surged through the streets in New Delhi and Madras, seeking targets for their anger.

Gandhi was driven to a nighttime rally here at a sports field after a long day of campaigning.

In sight of 10,000 people, he stepped from his bulletproof car into a throng of supporters who pressed garlands of flowers on him, according to reporters who witnessed the assassination.

Background As Gandhi walked on a red carpet to the speaker's platform, a concealed bomb exploded, almost at his feet. The powerful blast threw him to the ground and killed him instantly.

The bodies of nine other victims lay around him. They included seven police officers and two supporters. Dozens more were injured.

▼

Blast Rocks Trade Center

New York, February 27, 1993 (The Washington Times)—An apparent bomb blast in an underground garage rocked the 110-story World Trade Center yesterday, killing at least seven persons, injuring 600 and forcing thousands to flee down dark, smoke-filled stairways. The explosion, possibly set off by foreign terrorists, prompted law enforcement agencies to tighten security at the Capitol in Washington.

Background More than 50,000 people were evacuated from the World Trade Center during the hours immediately following the blast.

▲

The crater produced by the explosion was 150 feet across at its widest point and five stories deep.

▲

Three men use oxygen masks to aid their breathing after escaping following the explosion.

Background The terrorists had placed containers of Sarin, a deadly nerve gas, in subway stations and trains.

Hundreds in Japan Hunt Gas Attackers After 8 Die

Tokyo, Tuesday, March 21 (The New York Times)—A 300-member task force interrogated witnesses today and searched for clues as the Government appealed for public cooperation to prevent a repeat of the nerve gas attack by terrorists on the Tokyo subway system.

Eight people died and more than 4,700 others were treated in hospitals for that attack, which came at the peak of the Monday morning rush hour in one of the busiest commuter systems in the world.

The police appear concerned that the assault may not be the last, and they have stepped up security at train stations and airports around the country and are inspecting subway trashcans and platforms for suspicious objects.

No group has taken responsibility, and the police gave no indication today that they had any important developments in the case.

▲
Special chemical control unit members wearing anti-gas suits decontaminated the subway platforms following the terrorist attack.

Twelve people eventually died as a result of the attack. ▶

At Least 31 Are Dead, Scores Are Missing After Car Bomb Attack in Oklahoma City Wrecks a 9-Story Federal Office Building

Washington, April 19 (The New York Times)—The authorities opened an intensive hunt today for whoever bombed a federal office building in Oklahoma City, and proceeded on the theory that the bombing was a terrorist attack against the Government, law-enforcement officials said.

President Clinton appeared in the White House press room this afternoon and somberly promised the Government would hunt down the "evil cowards" responsible. "These people are killers," he said, "and must be treated like killers."

Background On April 19, 1995, just before 9:03 in the morning, there was a huge explosion outside the Alfred P. Murrah Federal Building in downtown Oklahoma City.

The explosion, which was the result of a massive truck bomb, left a 20-foot wide, 8-foot deep crater in the street. ▶

▲
The blast blew off the front side of the building, collapsing floors and burying victims under masses of concrete and steel. 168 people were killed by the explosion, and hundreds more were injured.

September 11, 2001

The Bombing of the World Trade Center, 1993

On February 26, 1993, a powerful truck bomb exploded in the underground parking garage of the World Trade Center in New York City. The bomb had been intended to topple one of the towers into the other and kill 250,000 people. Fortunately, this plan failed; however, 6 people were killed and extensive damage was done to the buildings.

A group of Islamic radicals was rounded up in the days following and found to be preparing gas and bomb attacks on a large variety of New York targets. The group's mastermind was Ramzi Yousef, who had left the United States on the day of the attack. He was eventually captured in 1995. Yousef's accomplices were a group of followers of the Egyptian Sheikh Omar Abd al-Rahman, the spiritual leader of Egypt's largest militant group, which has joined Osama bin Laden in recent years in calling for attacks on Americans.

Yousef provided the link between Abd al-Rahman's devoted followers and the money and terrorist know-how of Osama bin

Laden's al-Qaeda group. The investigation of the bombing was described in an Interpol[1] report.

On 26th February 1993, at approximately 12:18 P.M., an improvised explosive device exploded on the second level of the World Trade Center[2] parking basement.

The resulting blast produced a crater, approximately 150 feet in diameter and five floors deep, in the parking basement. The device had been placed in the rear cargo portion of a one-ton Ford F-350 Econoline van, owned by the Ryder Rental Agency, Jersey City, New Jersey. Approximately 6,800 tons of material were displaced by the blast. . . . The main explosive charge consisted primarily of approximately 200 to 1,500 pounds of a homemade fertilizer-based explosive, urea nitrate. . . . The resulting explosion killed six people and injured more than a thousand. More than 50,000 people were evacuated from the Trade Center complex during the hours immediately following the blast.

The initial inspection on 27th February was described as "a scene of massive devastation, almost **surreal**."[3] It was like walking into a cave, with no lights other than flashlights flickering across the crater. There were small pockets of fire, electrical arcing from damaged wiring, and automobile alarms whistling, howling and honking. The explosion ruptured two of the main sewage lines from both Trade towers and the Vista Hotel and several water mains from the air conditioning system. In all, more than 2 million gallons of water and sewage were pumped out of the crime scene.

---

[1] Interpol—short for the International Criminal Police Organization, an organization that fosters cooperation between the police forces of its roughly 125 member nations to catch international criminals.

[2] World Trade Center—formerly located near Wall Street in New York City, this central complex for business and government offices involved in international trade was opened in 1972. Each of its twin towers, which were destroyed in a terrorist attack in September 2001, was 110 stories tall.

[3] **surreal**—having an oddly dreamlike quality.

Once the type and amount of explosive had been estimated, it was possible to surmise that the bomb had been too large to transport in a sedan-type automobile, while the ceiling clearance limited the height of the vehicle. By this method of reasonable deduction, the initial opinion was that the explosive device had to have been transported into the Trade Center parking area in either a pickup truck or a van.

On 28th February, four FBI forensic chemists and four ATF[4] chemists arrived to begin explosive residue collection. During the early morning hours of this residue collection, the bomb technician discovered a fragment from a vehicle frame which displayed massive explosive damage. The ATF agent and bomb technician placed the 300-pound fragment on a litter and carried it to a police vehicle. The fragment was transported to the Laboratory for analysis. Due to sewage contamination, the piece was of no value for explosive residue analysis. A closer inspection of the fragment displayed a dot matrix number. The number was identified as the confidential vehicle identification number of a van reported stolen the day before the bombing. The vehicle was a 1990 Ford, F-350 Econoline van owned by the Ryder Rental Agency, rented in New Jersey and reported stolen in New Jersey. The frame fragment displayed explosive damage consistent with damage from a device exploding inside the vehicle.

FBI agents traveled to the Ryder Rental Agency in Jersey City, New Jersey, which had rented out the vehicle and began an interview of the station manager. While the interview was under way, an individual by the name of Mohammad Salameh telephoned Ryder and wanted his security deposit returned. A meeting was arranged so that Salameh would return to the Ryder Agency on

---

[4] ATF—Bureau of Alcohol, Tobacco, and Firearms; agency that enforces Federal laws relating to explosives.

4th March. When he returned for the $400 deposit, F B I agents were on hand to place him under surveillance. As Salameh was leaving, numerous media personnel were observed outside, setting up their photography equipment. It was then decided that Salameh would be arrested on the spot. His arrest and the subsequent search of his personal property led to Nidel Ayyad, a chemist working for the Allied Signal Corporation in New Jersey. Ayyad was connected to Salameh through telephone toll records and joint bank accounts. At the time of Ayyad's arrest his personal computer was seized from his office (more about that later). Also through toll records and receipts, a safe house or bomb factory was located on Pamrappo Avenue, in Jersey City. A search of this bomb factory revealed that acids and other chemicals had been used at that apartment to manufacture explosives. Traces of nitro-glycerine and urea nitrate were found on the carpet and embedded in the ceiling. It appeared that a chemical reaction involving acid had occurred in the apartment. At the same time, telephone toll records from Salameh and Ayyad showed that calls had been made to a self-storage center not too far from the bomb factory.

On 3rd March, a typewritten communication was received at *The New York Times*. The communiqué claimed responsibility for the bombing of the World Trade Center in the name of Allah.[5] The letter was composed on a personal computer and printed on a laser printer. Very little can be identified as to the origin of the printer, but a search of the hidden files in Ayyad's computer revealed wording identical to that of the text of the communiqué. Saliva samples from Salameh, Ayyad and a third man, Mahmud Abuhalima, were obtained and compared with the saliva on the envelope flap. A

---

[5] Allah—standard word for "God" in the Arabic language; the term is used by Arab Christians as well as Muslims.

DNA[6] Q Alpha examination concluded that Ayyad had licked the envelope on the communiqué received by the *Times*. Abuhalima, who was an integral part of the conspiracy, had fled the United States the day after the bombing, and had later been arrested in Egypt and **extradited**[7] back to the United States.

In September 1992, a man named Ahmad M. Ajaj had entered the United States from Pakistan at New York's JFK airport. He was arrested on a passport violation. In his checked luggage, Ajaj had numerous manuals and videocassette tapes. These tapes and manuals described methods of manufacturing explosives, including urea nitrate, nitro-glycerine, lead azide, TNT and other high explosives.

Interviews and latent fingerprint examinations identified two other individuals who were an integral part of the bombing conspiracy. The first, Ramzi Yousef, had entered the U.S. on the same flight as Ajaj, but had been deported immediately. Yousef was identified through fingerprints and photo spreads as having been associating with Salameh immediately prior to the bombing. His fingerprints were also found in the explosive manuals located in Ajaj's checked luggage. The second individual, known only as "Yassin," was identified in much the same manner and was probably involved in the packaging and delivery of the bomb on the morning of 26th February.

The FBI Laboratory was under the gun to complete all scientific examinations by 7th July 1993 in compliance with the Speedy Trial Act. A trial date was established for 6th September 1993.

---

[6] DNA—short for deoxyribonucleic acid, a unique sequence of proteins in human cells that can be used to "fingerprint" an individual.

[7] **extradited**—delivered to the legal jurisdiction of another government or authority.

During the six-month trial, more than 200 witnesses introduced over 1000 exhibits. On 4th March 1994, exactly one year after Salameh's arrest, the jury found Salameh, Ajaj, Abuhalima and Ayyad guilty on all thirty-eight counts.

QUESTIONS TO CONSIDER

1. Why do you think the scene of destruction was described as "almost surreal"?

2. What were some of the steps undertaken by those who investigated the bombing?

3. How did the FBI apprehend the first suspect in the case?

4. What is your opinion of the ability of these terrorists?

5. How was the 1993 bombing similar to the attack on the World Trade Center in September 2001?

Osama bin Laden

Most Islamic extremism of the last decade has been carried out by men who fought in the 1980s in Afghanistan's ten-year war against Soviet invaders. Muslims from around the world joined the Afghan mujahideen (Arabic, "fighters in a jihad," or holy war) in their struggle against the Soviets. One of the leading organizers of these Muslim guerrilla fighters was Osama bin Laden, a member of a rich family in Saudi Arabia. Bin Laden strongly opposes the Saudi government, believing the royal family to be bad Muslims and unfit guardians for Mecca and Medina, Islam's holy sites. Bin Laden was also angered by the use of Saudi territory by American troops during the 1991 Gulf War against Iraq. Saudi Arabia and Iraq are the lands where Islam was born and where its cultural heritage was created. The stationing of U.S. troops in Saudi Arabia and continuing U.S. actions against Iraq have made America bin Laden's new target. He turned his organization for recruiting mujahideen into al-Qaeda (Arabic, "the base"), a network for recruiting, financing, and training terrorists. His goal is to unite the many radical Islamic organizations around the world into a loose-knit alliance that can fight the West. In 1998, bin Laden issued a fatwa (Arabic, "religious ruling") calling on all Muslims to attack Americans. "The Spider in the Web," a September 2001 article from The Economist *that traces bin Laden's career, is followed by the text of the fatwa.*

The Spider in the Web

To millions of people in the western world, he has come to be viewed as the personification of evil. On the streets of Cairo, in the mountains of northern Pakistan, and even in the air-conditioned luxury of his native Saudi Arabia, he has many admirers, both open and secret.

But for foes and supporters alike, there is much about Osama bin Laden, the man at the center of a network of Islamist violence spanning 40 countries, that remains **enigmatic**[1] and contradictory. He was born in the heart of Saudi Arabia's privileged elite, but is now its harshest critic. As a young man, he became a popular figure within that elite because of his prominent role in the American-backed effort to **succor**[2] the rebels who were battling Soviet forces in Afghanistan. But for at least the past 11 years—since American troops arrived in his country to wrest control of Kuwait[3] from the Iraqis, and then stayed on after that war was won—he has regarded the United States and its allies with unqualified hatred.

His own religious roots are in the Sunni[4] branch of Islam, and some of his followers have a history of bitter conflict with followers of Shia[5] Islam, whose biggest stronghold is Iran. But he has insisted that differences within the Islamic world should be set aside for the sake of the broader struggle against western and Jewish interests. American officials say there is clear evidence of tactical co-operation between his organization, al-Qaeda, the government of Iran, and Iran's proxies in Lebanon,

---

[1] **enigmatic**—puzzling.

[2] **succor**—aid.

[3] Kuwait—country in the Arabian Peninsula at the head of the Persian Gulf. Iraq invaded and occupied the country in 1990, sparking the Persian Gulf War, which ended with Iraqi troops being driven out by a coalition of Arab and Western forces.

[4] Sunni—larger of the two main branches of Islam.

[5] Shia—smaller branch of Islam whose members acknowledge Ali, Muhammad's son-in-law, and his descendants as the rightful successors of Muhammad.

the Hezbollah[6] group. From the early 1990s, members of his group and its Egyptian allies were being sent to Lebanon to receive training from Hezbollah: an unusual example of Sunni-Shia co-operation in the broader anti-western struggle.

Thousands of would-be Islamist fighters from at least a dozen countries have received training at camps which he set up, at first in Sudan and, since 1996, in Afghanistan. But by no means all the beneficiaries of this training are under his control. And, to judge from the evidence that has emerged from three big trials in America over the past decade, many of the people who implement his plans have little idea who their ultimate boss may be.

Mr. bin Laden was born in Riyadh in 1957, the 17th of the 52 children of Saudi Arabia's most successful building magnate.[7] His father, Mohammed bin Oud bin Laden, came from southern Yemen in 1932, when the kingdom's new dynasty was installed, and rose from humble beginnings to become the favored building contractor to the royal house.

The bin Laden group is still the kingdom's biggest construction business, with a turnover of tens of billions of dollars. Its latest projects include airport facilities in Kuala Lumpur, a runway in Cairo and a vast new mosque in Medina. Its recent investments have included a marble factory in Italy and a share in Iridium, a troubled satellite consortium.

How much of this fortune has flowed into Mr. bin Laden's coffers? According to the State Department's list of terrorist organizations, he is "said to have inherited approximately $300M." But others who know the Saudi royal house say this is a wild exaggeration. Since the early

---

[6] Hezbollah—"Party of God," Islamic fundamentalist group in Lebanon and other Muslim countries. Fundamentalists believe in strict observance of religious principles.

[7] magnate—powerful and influential person, especially in business.

1990s, he has been estranged from his family and from the Saudi government, which revoked his citizenship in 1994. The Saudi authorities have frozen his bank accounts and his share of the bin Laden fortune has been confiscated.

Some of the money lost then has, however, been replenished. Former officials of the C I A and the F B I say Mr. bin Laden has been receiving secret donations from rich well-wishers in the Middle East and from Islamic charitable organizations. He may also take a cut from the Taliban's[8] sales of opium. Units of his organization are believed to raise money through financial and other sorts of crime. For example, Ahmed Ressam, an Algerian who plotted to bomb Los Angeles airport but later co-operated with American authorities, says he was given $12,000 of seed-money to set up his operation. When he asked for more cash, he was advised to finance himself by credit-card fraud.

What marks out Mr. bin Laden from other godfathers of violence against western and Israeli targets is the extraordinary breadth of his connections. Bridging personal rivalries and **ideological**[9] differences, he is prepared to make tactical alliances with almost any group that shares his aims: the "liberation" of his country and region from American troops, the replacement of pro-western regimes by militant Islamist ones, the defeat of Israel and the restoration of Muslim control over the holy places of Jerusalem.

Unlike many members of the Saudi elite, Mr. bin Laden was never educated in the West, nor even at a western-run college in the Middle East. His only exposure to a cosmopolitan, western way of life was the two

---

[8] Taliban—political and military group in Afghanistan that takes its name from the Farsi (Persian) word for "students"; many of its members were trained in Islamic fundamentalism in Pakistan. Appearing first in 1994, this extremely conservative faction controlled almost all of Afghanistan by 2001 despite worldwide disapproval of its social policies. It was overthrown by the American-backed Northern Alliance in late 2001.

[9] **ideological**—of or relating to ideology: ideas, usually related to social power and politics.

years he spent in the **hedonistic**[10] atmosphere of Beirut after leaving school in 1973. While his brothers studied abroad, he took his degree in engineering in his home city of Jeddah; and he may perhaps have been influenced by the view of conservative clerics that Beirut's plunge into bloody civil war was a divine punishment for its decadent way of life.

Like tens of thousands of idealistic Muslims—and others—from all over the world, he seemed to find his vocation in the battle being waged by the mujahideen, a broad coalition of Islamic fighters divided into at least seven factions, against the Soviet forces that invaded Afghanistan in December 1979. He was uniquely well-placed to act as a **conduit**[11] between the mujahideen and the kingdom because of his family's fortune and his personal contacts with the Saudi elite, including Prince Turki bin Faisal bin Abdelaziz, who was the Saudi intelligence chief for 24 years until his abrupt and unexplained dismissal a few weeks ago.

Shuttling between Peshawar, the Pakistani base for the mujahideen, and Saudi Arabia, Mr. bin Laden raised huge sums of money and established a "services office" (maktab al-khidamat) which recruited fighters from all over the world—including the United States, where his men operated from an office in Brooklyn. According to American legal documents, the services office had **metamorphosed**[12]—as early as 1989, the year the Russians left Afghanistan—into al-Qaeda, "the base," which forms the core of Mr. bin Laden's network of Islamist violence.

As a supplier of the Afghan rebels, Mr. bin Laden was **indefatigable**.[13] As well as procuring weapons and humanitarian aid, he obtained bulldozers and engineering equipment which were used to drive tunnels

---

[10] **hedonistic**—pleasure-loving.

[11] **conduit**—channel.

[12] **metamorphosed**—transformed.

[13] **indefatigable**—tireless.

through the mountains of Afghanistan. Although most of his help was logistical and financial, he also saw some combat. In 1996 he was involved in the defense of a small village called Jadji, and in 1989 he was spotted by John Simpson, a British writer and broadcaster, among the forces besieging Jalalabad.

Support for the mujahideen was closely orchestrated between the governments and secret services of the United States, Britain, Pakistan and Saudi Arabia. A privileged recipient of American and Saudi aid (distributed by the Pakistanis) was the militant Islamic leader Gulbuddin Hikmatyar, with whom Mr. bin Laden, in turn, was closely associated. The privileged treatment of Mr. Hikmatyar—regarded as power-hungry and fanatical by other rebel groups—was viewed with some bafflement in the **expatriate**[14] community in Peshawar, and it led to backroom arguments between American officials and their British partners.

Was there any privileged relationship between Mr. bin Laden and the Americans? British officials with knowledge of **covert**[15] operations in support of the Afghan rebels believed there was such a relationship, although this has been vigorously denied by their American counterparts. In any case, soon after the Soviet withdrawal from Afghanistan in 1989, Mr. bin Laden became disillusioned with his **erstwhile**[16] friends in America, Britain and the Saudi elite. He was dismayed by American support for Dr. Sayid Mohammed Najibullah, an Afghan leader whom he viewed as a Russian stooge; and he bitterly opposed the arrival of American troops in Saudi Arabia in August 1990.

Emboldened by the prestige he had acquired as a powerful friend of the mujahideen, he became

---

[14] **expatriate**—relating to a citizen of one country who takes up residence in another country.

[15] **covert**—secret.

[16] **erstwhile**—former.

increasingly vocal in his criticism of the Saudi leadership—and an embarrassment to his friends and family. He was expelled from Saudi Arabia in 1991 and took refuge in Sudan, where he remained until that country, under international pressure, asked him to leave and return to Afghanistan, his old stamping ground.

Officials in America and Europe believe that stifling Mr. bin Laden's financial network would help to stop more attacks. But that will be difficult. Although it is possible to pinpoint and freeze accounts held in America and Europe, seizing assets held in the Middle East under names not directly related to Mr. bin Laden's organization is far harder. When Mr. bin Laden realized that intelligence agencies were pursuing his financial arrangements, he started to rely more heavily on cash, which leaves no trace. His global network may use an internal credit system similar to those employed by the Mafia and Triad gangs,[17] says Magnus Ranstorp, a terrorism expert at the University of St Andrews. Like cash, it leaves no audit trail. "We will never be able to cut off his funds entirely," says Mr. Cannistraro,[18] "only restrict them."

The biggest nightmare is that Mr. bin Laden and his associates will acquire, or have already acquired, biological, chemical or even nuclear weapons. American legal documents allege that his supporters have been looking for nuclear materials since the early 1990s. Another risk, says bin Laden-watcher Yonah Alexander, is that of devastating cyber-warfare.[19] And even if the man himself is somehow neutralized, plenty of militant Muslims will be ready to struggle on in his name—with or without direct orders from their hero.

---

[17] Triad gangs—Chinese criminal organizations.

[18] Mr. Cannistraro—Vincent Cannistraro, former CIA official who is an expert on terrorism.

[19] cyber-warfare—politically motivated attacks against information systems, computer systems, computer programs, and data.

Fatwa: *Jihad Against Jews and Crusaders*

Praise be to God, who revealed the Book,[20] controls the clouds, defeats factionalism, and says in His Book: "But when the forbidden months are past, then fight and slay the pagans wherever ye find them, seize them, beleaguer them, and lie in wait for them in every stratagem (of war)"; and peace be upon our Prophet, Muhammad Bin-'Abdallah,[21] who said: I have been sent with the sword between my hands to ensure that no one but God is worshipped, God who put my livelihood under the shadow of my spear and who inflicts humiliation and scorn on those who disobey my orders.

The Arabian Peninsula has never—since God made it flat, created its desert, and encircled it with seas—been stormed by any forces like the crusader[22] armies spreading in it like locusts, eating its riches and wiping out its plantations. All this is happening at a time in which nations are attacking Muslims like people fighting over a plate of food. In the light of the grave situation and the lack of support, we and you are obliged to discuss current events, and we should all agree on how to settle the matter.

No one argues today about three facts that are known to everyone; we will list them, in order to remind everyone:

First, for over seven years the United States has been occupying the lands of Islam in the holiest of places, the Arabian Peninsula, plundering its riches, dictating to its rulers, humiliating its people, terrorizing its neighbors, and turning its bases in the Peninsula into a spearhead through which to fight the neighboring Muslim peoples.

---

[20] Book—Islam's sacred text, the Quran.

[21] Muhammad Bin-'Abdallah—(c. 570–632) founder of Islam and the Muslim community. He recorded the Quran as it was revealed to him by Allah and is therefore viewed as his messenger.

[22] crusader—Western, particularly American. The *fatwa* likens modern Western armies to those that participated in the Crusades, a series of wars to capture the Holy Land from Muslims, launched in 1095 by European Christians.

If some people have in the past argued about the fact of the occupation, all the people of the Peninsula have now acknowledged it. The best proof of this is the Americans' continuing aggression against the Iraqi people using the Peninsula as a staging post, even though all its rulers are against their territories being used to that end, but they are helpless.

Second, despite the great devastation inflicted on the Iraqi people by the crusader-Zionist[23] alliance, and despite the huge number of those killed, which has exceeded 1 million . . . despite all this, the Americans are once again trying to repeat the horrific massacres, as though they are not content with the protracted blockade imposed after the ferocious war or the fragmentation and devastation.

So here they come to annihilate what is left of this people and to humiliate their Muslim neighbors.

Third, if the Americans' aims behind these wars are religious and economic, the aim is also to serve the Jews' petty state and divert attention from its occupation of Jerusalem and murder of Muslims there. The best proof of this is their eagerness to destroy Iraq, the strongest neighboring Arab state, and their endeavor to fragment all the states of the region such as Iraq, Saudi Arabia, Egypt, and Sudan into paper statelets and through their disunion and weakness to guarantee Israel's survival and the continuation of the brutal crusade occupation of the Peninsula.

All these crimes and sins committed by the Americans are a clear declaration of war on God, his messenger, and Muslims. And ulema[24] have throughout Islamic history

---

[23] Zionist—Israeli.

[24] ulema—or *ulama*, Arabic word for the social class that is especially learned in Islamic religion and sciences. Sometimes the term is used to refer to Muslim "priests," though there is no official priesthood in Islam. Throughout history, the opinions of the ulema have been sought by Muslim governments.

unanimously agreed that the jihad[25] is an individual duty if the enemy destroys the Muslim countries.

On that basis, and in compliance with God's order, we issue the following fatwa to all Muslims:

The ruling to kill the Americans and their allies—civilians and military—is an individual duty for every Muslim who can do it in any country in which it is possible to do it, in order to liberate the al-Aqsa Mosque and the holy mosque[26] from their grip, and in order for their armies to move out of all the lands of Islam, defeated and unable to threaten any Muslim.

We—with God's help—call on every Muslim who believes in God and wishes to be rewarded to comply with God's order to kill the Americans and plunder their money wherever and whenever they find it. We also call on Muslim ulema, leaders, youths, and soldiers to launch the raid on Satan's U.S. troops and the devil's supporters allying with them, and to displace those who are behind them so that they may learn a lesson.

---

[25] jihad—Arabic word for "fight" or "battle," it is a duty placed on Muslims and often translated as "holy war." Islam spells out four ways to fulfill jihad: by heart, tongue, hand, and sword. Sometimes these struggles are only religious or political in nature rather than involving outright warfare.

[26] al-Aqsa Mosque and the holy mosque—Islamic sacred places in Jerusalem and Mecca.

QUESTIONS TO CONSIDER

1. Why has Osama bin Laden been such an effective terrorist leader?

2. What are some of reasons that bin Laden hates the United States?

3. How does the article in The Economist suggest bin Laden can be stopped?

4. How does the *fatwa* present recent history in the Middle East?

5. How does the *fatwa* create an emotional response in the audience to which it is addressed?

The Attack

Early on Tuesday morning, September 11, 2001, radical Islamic ter-
rorists hijacked four planes that were en route from the East Coast
to the West. Two were flown into the World Trade Center towers in
New York City, one struck the Pentagon in Washington, D.C., and the
fourth was brought down in Pennsylvania by the plane's passengers.
The explosive power of the jet fuel in the planes caused the two
towers of the World Trade Center to catch on fire and eventually
collapse. An hour's delay saved the lives of thousands of people who
work in the buildings, but nearly four hundred police and firefighters
were killed later when the two towers fell. New York City came to a
standstill. The bridges and tunnels were closed to traffic, the subway
and buses did not run for much of the day, and the lower part of
the city was covered with dense smoke. In the following selection,
four well-known writers react to different aspects of the attack: the
novelist Colson Whitehead describes his reaction to seeing the Towers
collapse from Brooklyn; the novelist Stephen King describes the
simplicity of the tools the terrorists used to create such destruction;
the novelist Jennifer Egan describes how September 11 reminded
us that, although we are all connected by the new communication
technology, we still cannot always rescue those we love; and the
essayist Judith Shulevitz describes how tragedy rivets our attention
with its excitement as well as its horrors.

The Image

by Colson Whitehead

Fort Greene Park in Brooklyn has hills that look out on Lower Manhattan. On the morning of Sept. 11, people were staked out in small groups, strangers trading misinformation and speculation. What was sure and known was that the towers were burning; we could see that from the northern slope of the park. The trees at the edge below us obscure all but the highest landmarks: the tips of the Manhattan Bridge, the roofs of the more ambitious corporate headquarters. The top halves of the twin towers had always overpowered the scene like bullies.

We picked out a spot, and I told my wife, "You should take a picture." Because it was a very nice shot, well composed. The three men in the foreground were obviously strangers, standing together, but not so close as to violate any rules about personal space. They were of different races; one had a dog that looked away from the scene at a bird or something, one had abandoned a bicycle on the ground. The bicycle was a nice touch—couldn't have placed it better myself. In the sky before the men, the towers burned. The right part of the frame was unblemished blue sky, the left a great wash of brown and black smoke. The dynamic event, the small human figures. It was a nice shot. Call it "The Watchers" or "The Spectators." Frame it. Keep it away.

Then the wind shifted for a second, and where the second tower should have been, it wasn't. All that time, I had assumed that the smoke had merely hidden it, but it hadn't been there at all. And then Tower 2 sighed. The top floors buckled out, spraying tiny white **shards**,[1] and the building sank down into itself, crouching beneath the trees and out of frame. I shouted, "Oh, my God!" It had been a nice shot. And certainly it had been easier to

---

[1] **shards**—fragments, as of glass or metal.

shape the horror into an **aesthetic**[2] experience and deny the human reality. There was safety in that distance. A man picked up his bike and walked away. My wife and I went home. There had never been any safety at all.

The Weapon
by Stephen King

People keep saying "like a movie," "like a book," "like a war zone," and I keep thinking: No, not at all like a movie or a book—that's no computer-generated image, because you can't see any wash or blur in the background. This is what it really looks like when an actual plane filled with actual human beings and loaded with jet fuel hits a skyscraper. This is the truth.

Certainly, it seems to me that the idea of an enormous intelligence breakdown is **ludicrous**;[3] again, this was not like a book, not like a movie; this was men armed with nothing but knives and box cutters relying on simple speed to keep people off balance long enough to accomplish their goals. In the case of the plane that crashed in Pennsylvania, they failed. With the other three, however, they succeeded quite nicely. Cost of weaponry? Based on what we know now, less than $100. This qualifies them as cut-rate, low-tech, stealth guerrillas flying well under the radar of American intelligence. We must realize this and grasp an even more difficult truth: although it is comforting to have a bogyman, and every child's party needs a paper donkey to pin the tall on, this Osama bin Laden fellow may not have been the guy responsible. It wouldn't hurt to remember that the boys who shot up Columbine High School planned to finish their day by hijacking a jetliner and flying it into—yes, that's right—the World Trade Center. Dylan Klebold

---

[2] **aesthetic**—relating to the appreciation of beauty.

[3] **ludicrous**—laughable because of obvious absurdity; ridiculous.

and Eric Harris[4] weren't exactly rocket scientists, and the guys who did this didn't have to be either. All you had to be was willing to die, and these guys were. It could happen again. And now that crazos the world over see that it's possible to get 72 hours of uninterrupted air time on a budget, it will almost certainly happen again.

The Technology
by Jennifer Egan

I first learned of trouble at the World Trade Center from my husband, who watched the second plane's explosion from inside a Q train on the Manhattan Bridge. He reached me at home on his cell phone. It was only after we had hung up that the thought of him suspended there, above the East River in a subway car, began to unsettle me. Still, I felt curiously calm. He's fine, I thought. After all, I just talked to him.

Of course, that was no guarantee of anything. Throughout the disasters of Sept. 11, people harnessed communications technology from the most extreme circumstances imaginable. Barbara Olson, a passenger on American Airlines Flight 757, used her cell phone to report early details of the hijacking. Friends and families of workers in the World Trade Center used e-mail to exhort their loved ones to flee the building. Some of those trapped in the rubble used their pagers or cell phones to call for rescue. The sheer density of such exchanges makes the boundary between those inside and outside Tuesday's disasters seem difficult to establish.

Still, there is an eerie poignancy about those high-tech goodbyes from people trapped inside burning buildings and runaway planes. A similar quality clung to the story of Rob Hall, the leader of a doomed 1996

---

[4] Columbine High School . . . Dylan Klebold and Eric Harris—On April 20, 1999, Dylan Klebold and Eric Harris, two students at Columbine High School in Littleton, Colorado, shot and killed twelve fellow students and a teacher.

expedition up Mount Everest. Marooned in a snow-storm, Hall reached his pregnant wife in New Zealand by radiophone, and together they chose a name for their unborn child. The imbalance is almost crushing: if they could hear each other's voices, name a child, say good-bye, how could he not have been rescued?

We in the developed world have come a long way toward eliminating time and space as determining factors in our lives. We can whisper into the ear of someone across the globe. We can trade intimacies with people whose whereabouts are unknown to us—beside the point, even. Without a doubt, Tuesday's tragedies showcase the extraordinary rewards of the communications revolution. Yet never have the limits of communication been more stark. One person is inside a burning building and one is outside. Their voices may meet in the digital void,[5] but they can't pull each other to safety across it.

Real War
by Judith Shulevitz

So this is what it's like to go to war, real war, in which real Americans die and tolerance for people with dangerous ideas seems frivolous compared with the need to stop them. Just a couple of weeks ago, I would have dismissed the exchange of civil liberties for safety as a false trade-off. But then I didn't know what it felt like to see even network news anchors grow nervous inside their New York skyscrapers. Every other American-fought war taking place during my adulthood has felt, by comparison, like a media event. Grenada?[6]

---

[5] digital void—empty space in which computer-based communication takes place; cyberspace.

[6] Grenada—small-scale American military operation in October 1983 in which U.S. Marines invaded the tiny Caribbean island of Grenada, unseated the leaders of a group that had recently overthrown the Grenadan government, and set up a government favorable to the United States.

The Gulf War? Army exercises and fireworks displays, with the same relationship to national defense as a burlesque extravaganza has to romantic intimacy. Now I understand the urgent patriotism Steven Spielberg was trying to get across in "Band of Brothers,"[7] in retrospect the most **prescient**[8] television program of the days before the attack.

This sense of seriousness, of having a role to play in history, is why war engenders so much nostalgia despite its atrocities. Somewhere deep in my heart, I have always longed for a catastrophe like the present one. Such wishes may seem appalling once they have come true, but we harbor them nonetheless. The novelist Don DeLillo[9] has called this our "tone of enthusiasm for runaway calamity." I have sometimes imagined, while panting up a mountain, that I'm sneaking away from a ghetto to join some partisans in the forest. Others dress up in Civil War uniforms and reproduce historic battles, or just watch the History Channel.

The desire for a collective purpose seems almost as great as the desire for a personal one. Indeed, if you ask people who have lived through periods of intense national challenge—veterans of World War II, of course, or of the Czechoslovakian Velvet Revolution[10]—about the high points of their lives, you might conclude that they value their memories of struggle more than those of peace. There's nothing like being under attack to clarify what's important and to sweep away the nonsense on which we tend to squander our public attention: petty political squabbling, the enervating celebrity gossip.

---

[7] Steven Spielberg ... "Band of Brothers"—In the fall of 2001, the HBO television network broadcast a 10-part miniseries produced by Steven Spielberg about the experiences of an American army unit during World War II.

[8] **prescient**—anticipating the future; far-seeing.

[9] Don DeLillo—(1936–) American novelist known for fictional studies of U.S. history.

[10] Czechoslovakian Velvet Revolution—In November 1989, massive protests in Czechoslovakia resulted in the sudden collapse of Communist rule there.

Never again to have to think about Gary Condit or Britney Spears![11] To focus as a nation on our future and that of our children! These are instinctively attractive and ennobling ideas. Only once those other topics disappear, if they disappear, do we begin to appreciate how lucky we had been to be obsessed by them.

---

[11] Gary Condit or Britney Spears—Gary Condit is a U.S. Representative from California who was given a great deal of attention by the media in the summer of 2001 because of his alleged involvement with a young female aide who had been missing since April. Britney Spears is a pop singer.

QUESTIONS TO CONSIDER

1. What does Colson Whitehead mean when he says, "There had never been any safety at all"?

2. Why does Stephen King think that the events of September 11 were not "like a movie" or "like a book"?

3. What irony about the effect of our sophisticated communications technology is noted by Jennifer Egan?

4. Why does Judith Shulevitz think that we are drawn to calamity?

5. All of these writers are reacting to the events of September 11 in a very personal way. What do you think is the appropriate way for writers to react to a national tragedy like the terrorist attacks? What would you have written if asked to comment in the week after September 11?

Why Do They Hate Us?

BY FAREED ZAKARIA

The attacks on the World Trade Center and the Pentagon on September 11, 2001, were directed against innocent civilians. Americans have been forced to ask themselves why they are the target of such extreme violence. Many reasons have been put forward, from America's wealth and political liberty to its support of Israel and the attacks on Iraq. But perhaps the things the United States has not done have weighed more than the things done. U.S. relations with the Middle East were mostly formed during the Cold War, when how a government stood in relation to America's struggle with communism was far more important than if it provided the basic needs of health, education, law, and economic freedom to its population. During the Cold War, as generation after generation of Muslims grew up with crippling poverty and hopelessness, they were told that it was due to the oppression of the West and of America in particular. In a Newsweek *article published in October 2001, foreign affairs expert Fareed Zakaria examines some of the ways the United States has made enemies in the Muslim world.*

To the question "Why do the terrorists hate us?" Americans could be pardoned for answering, "Why should we care?" The immediate reaction to the murder of 5,000 innocents is anger, not analysis. Yet anger will not be enough to get us through what is sure to be a long struggle. For that we will need answers.

The ones we have heard so far have been comforting but familiar. We stand for freedom and they hate it. We are rich and they envy us. We are strong and they resent this. All of which is true. But there are billions of poor and weak and oppressed people around the world. They don't turn planes into bombs. They don't blow themselves up to kill thousands of civilians. If envy were the cause of terrorism, Beverly Hills, Fifth Avenue, and Mayfair would have become morgues long ago. There is something stronger at work here than deprivation and jealousy. Something that can move men to kill but also to die. Osama bin Laden has an answer—religion. For him and his followers, this is a holy war between Islam and the Western world. Most Muslims disagree. Every Islamic country in the world has condemned the attacks of Sept. 11. To many, bin Laden belongs to a long line of extremists who have invoked religion to justify mass murder and spur men to suicide. The words "thug," "zealot" and "assassin" all come from ancient terror cults—Hindu, Jewish and Muslim, respectively—that believed they were doing the work of God. The terrorist's mind is its own place, and like Milton's Satan,[1] can make a hell of heaven, a heaven of hell. Whether it is the Unabomber,[2] Aum Shinrikyo,[3] or Baruch Goldstein (who killed scores of unarmed Muslims in Hebron), terrorists

---

[1] Milton's Satan—hero of the epic poem *Paradise Lost* by the English poet John Milton (1608–1674), which details Satan's revolt against God.

[2] Unabomber—name given to serial bomber Theodore J. Kaczynski, whose 17-year campaign of mailing explosive devices to university professors and business executives killed 3 people and injured 23. He was arrested in 1996 and imprisoned in 1997.

[3] Aum Shinrikyo—Buddhism-based Japanese religious sect founded in 1987 by Shoko Asahara. The group achieved worldwide infamy in 1995 when thousands were injured and 12 people died after sect members released nerve gas into a Tokyo subway.

are almost always misfits who place their own twisted morality above mankind's.

But bin Laden and his followers are not an isolated cult like Aum Shinrikyo or the Branch Davidians[4] or demented loners like Timothy McVeigh[5] and the Unabomber. They come out of a culture that reinforces their hostility, distrust and hatred of the West—and of America in particular. This culture does not condone terrorism but fuels the **fanaticism**[6] that is at its heart. To say that al-Qaeda is a fringe group may be reassuring, but it is false. Read the Arab press in the aftermath of the attacks and you will detect a not-so-hidden admiration for bin Laden. Or consider this from the Pakistani newspaper *The Nation*: "September 11 was not mindless terrorism for terrorism's sake. It was reaction and revenge, even retribution." Why else is America's response to the terror attacks so deeply constrained by fears of an "Islamic backlash" on the streets? Pakistan will dare not allow Washington use of its bases. Saudi Arabia trembles at the thought of having to help us publicly. Egypt pleads that our strikes be as limited as possible. The problem is not that Osama bin Laden believes that this is a religious war against America. It's that millions of people across the Islamic world seem to agree.

---

[4] Branch Davidians—religious group that is an offshoot of the Davidian Seventh-day Adventist (SDA) Church with a focus on preparing for the return of Jesus as outlined in the Bible. Led by David Koresh beginning in 1986, it lost 80 members when the FBI fired flammable material into its Waco, Texas, headquarters after four federal agents died in an attempt to end a standoff with the sect.

[5] Timothy McVeigh—McVeigh was executed in 2001 for his role in the bombing of a federal building in Oklahoma City in 1995 that left 168 people dead. The worst case of domestic terrorism in U.S. history was motivated, McVeigh claimed, by a desire to avenge deaths that had occurred exactly two years earlier, when federal agents raided the compound of the Branch Davidians in Waco, Texas.

[6] **fanaticism**—extreme devotion to a belief or cause.

QUESTIONS TO CONSIDER

1. Why do you think some Muslims might agree with a "holy war" on Western nations while most do not?

2. What does the author mean by stating that a "terrorist's mind . . . can make a hell of heaven, a heaven of hell"?

3. What is the author's point in mentioning that the words *thug, zealot* and *assassin* originated in different religious cultures?

4. Why might the type of terrorists who follow Osama bin Laden be easier—or harder—to deal with than the "isolated cults" or "demented loners" with whom they are compared?

Address to the Nation

BY PRESIDENT GEORGE W. BUSH

The immediate reaction of Americans to the September 11 attacks was confusion. The unthinkable had happened and fears ran wild. President George W. Bush spoke to the nation both that morning and in the evening, declaring the attacks acts of war. In the days that followed, the President met the challenge by committing America to defending itself by striking out at both terrorists and the nations that harbor and defend them. On September 20, he delivered an address to the nation that drew attention to the courage of many Americans in the wake of the attacks, to the worldwide outpouring of sympathy and horror, and to the resolve of Americans to fight a long and difficult war against terrorism.

Mr. Speaker, Mr. President Pro Tempore, members of Congress, and fellow Americans:

In the normal course of events, Presidents come to this chamber to report on the state of the Union. Tonight, no such report is needed. It has already been delivered by the American people.

We have seen it in the courage of passengers, who rushed terrorists to save others on the ground—passengers like an exceptional man named Todd Beamer. And would you please help me to welcome his wife, Lisa Beamer, here tonight.

We have seen the state of our Union in the endurance of rescuers, working past exhaustion. We have seen the unfurling of flags, the lighting of candles, the giving of blood, the saying of prayers—in English, Hebrew, and Arabic. We have seen the decency of a loving and giving people who have made the grief of strangers their own.

My fellow citizens, for the last nine days, the entire world has seen for itself the state of our Union—and it is strong.

Tonight we are a country awakened to danger and called to defend freedom. Our grief has turned to anger, and anger to resolution. Whether we bring our enemies to justice, or bring justice to our enemies, justice will be done.

I thank the Congress for its leadership at such an important time. . . .

And on behalf of the American people, I thank the world for its outpouring of support. America will never forget the sounds of our National Anthem playing at Buckingham Palace, on the streets of Paris, and at Berlin's Brandenburg Gate.

We will not forget South Korean children gathering to pray outside our embassy in Seoul, or the prayers of sympathy offered at a **mosque**[1] in Cairo. We will not forget moments of silence and days of mourning in Australia and Africa and Latin America.

Nor will we forget the citizens of 80 other nations who died with our own: dozens of Pakistanis; more than 130 Israelis; more than 250 citizens of India; men and

---

[1] **mosque**—Muslim house of worship.

women from El Salvador, Iran, Mexico and Japan; and hundreds of British citizens. America has no truer friend than Great Britain. . . .

On September the 11th, enemies of freedom committed an act of war against our country. Americans have known wars—but for the past 136 years, they have been wars on foreign soil, except for one Sunday in 1941. Americans have known the casualties of war—but not at the center of a great city on a peaceful morning. Americans have known surprise attacks—but never before on thousands of civilians. All of this was brought upon us in a single day—and night fell on a different world, a world where freedom itself is under attack.

Americans have many questions tonight. Americans are asking: Who attacked our country? The evidence we have gathered all points to a collection of loosely affiliated terrorist organizations known as al-Qaeda. They are the same murderers indicted for bombing American embassies in Tanzania and Kenya, and responsible for bombing the U.S.S. *Cole.*

Al-Qaeda is to terror what the mafia is to crime. But its goal is not making money; its goal is remaking the world—and imposing its radical beliefs on people everywhere.

The terrorists practice a fringe form of Islamic **extremism**[2] that has been rejected by Muslim scholars and the vast majority of Muslim **clerics**[3]—a fringe movement that perverts the peaceful teachings of Islam. The terrorists' directive commands them to kill Christians and Jews, to kill all Americans, and make no distinction among military and civilians, including women and children.

This group and its leader—a person named Osama bin Laden—are linked to many other organizations in

---

[2] **extremism**—policy or political philosophy that advocates or resorts to measures beyond the norm.

[3] **clerics**—members of the clergy, a body of officials who perform religious services—such as priests, ministers, or rabbis.

different countries, including the Egyptian Islamic Jihad[4] and the Islamic Movement of Uzbekistan.[5] There are thousands of these terrorists in more than 60 countries. They are recruited from their own nations and neighborhoods and brought to camps in places like Afghanistan, where they are trained in the tactics of terror. They are sent back to their homes or sent to hide in countries around the world to plot evil and destruction.

The leadership of al-Qaeda has great influence in Afghanistan and supports the Taliban regime in controlling most of that country. In Afghanistan, we see al-Qaeda's vision for the world.

Afghanistan's people have been brutalized—many are starving and many have fled. Women are not allowed to attend school. You can be jailed for owning a television. Religion can be practiced only as their leaders dictate. A man can be jailed in Afghanistan if his beard is not long enough.

The United States respects the people of Afghanistan—after all, we are currently its largest source of humanitarian aid—but we condemn the Taliban regime. It is not only repressing its own people, it is threatening people everywhere by sponsoring and sheltering and supplying terrorists. By aiding and **abetting**[6] murder, the Taliban regime is committing murder.

And tonight, the United States of America makes the following demands on the Taliban: Deliver to United States authorities all the leaders of al-Qaeda who hide in your land. Release all foreign nationals, including American citizens, you have unjustly imprisoned. Protect foreign journalists, diplomats and aid workers in your country. Close immediately and permanently every

---

[4] Islamic Jihad—fundamentalist group that has used terrorism to disrupt the peace process between Israel and the Palestinians.

[5] Islamic Movement of Uzbekistan—coalition of anti-Western and anti-Israeli Islamic militants from Uzbekistan and other Central Asian states.

[6] **abetting**—aiding in criminal activity.

terrorist training camp in Afghanistan, and hand over every terrorist, and every person in their support structure, to appropriate authorities. Give the United States full access to terrorist training camps, so we can make sure they are no longer operating.

These demands are not open to negotiation or discussion. The Taliban must act, and act immediately. They will hand over the terrorists, or they will share in their fate.

I also want to speak tonight directly to Muslims throughout the world. We respect your faith. It's practiced freely by many millions of Americans, and by millions more in countries that America counts as friends. Its teachings are good and peaceful, and those who commit evil in the name of Allah **blaspheme**[7] the name of Allah. The terrorists are traitors to their own faith, trying, in effect, to hijack Islam itself. The enemy of America is not our many Muslim friends; it is not our many Arab friends. Our enemy is a radical network of terrorists, and every government that supports them.

Our war on terror begins with al-Qaeda, but it does not end there. It will not end until every terrorist group of global reach has been found, stopped and defeated.

Americans are asking: why do they hate us? They hate what we see right here in this chamber—a democratically elected government. Their leaders are self-appointed. They hate our freedoms—our freedom of religion, our freedom of speech, our freedom to vote and assemble and disagree with each other.

They want to overthrow existing governments in many Muslim countries, such as Egypt, Saudi Arabia, and Jordan. They want to drive Israel out of the Middle East. They want to drive Christians and Jews out of vast regions of Asia and Africa.

These terrorists kill not merely to end lives, but to disrupt and end a way of life. With every atrocity, they hope that America grows fearful, retreating from the

---

[7] **blaspheme**—speak of (God or something sacred) in a disrespectful way.

world and forsaking our friends. They stand against us, because we stand in their way.

We are not deceived by their pretenses to piety.[8] We have seen their kind before. They are the heirs of all the murderous ideologies of the 20th century. By sacrificing human life to serve their radical visions—by abandoning every value except the will to power—they follow in the path of fascism,[9] and Nazism,[10] and totalitarianism.[11] And they will follow that path all the way, to where it ends: in history's unmarked grave of discarded lies.

Americans are asking: How will we fight and win this war? We will direct every resource at our command— every means of diplomacy, every tool of intelligence, every instrument of law enforcement, every financial influence, and every necessary weapon of war—to the disruption and to the defeat of the global terror network.

This war will not be like the war against Iraq a decade ago, with a decisive liberation of territory and a swift conclusion. It will not look like the air war above Kosovo[12] two years ago, where no ground troops were used and not a single American was lost in combat.

Our response involves far more than instant retaliation and isolated strikes. Americans should not expect one battle, but a lengthy campaign, unlike any other we have ever seen. It may include dramatic strikes, visible on TV, and **covert**[13] operations, secret even in success.

---

[8] pretenses to piety—false claims of religious devotion.

[9] fascism—political philosophy that advocates a strong, centralized nationalistic government headed by a powerful dictator.

[10] Nazism—fascist policies of the National Socialist German Workers party in the 1930s and 1940s; its ideas are based on totalitarianism, a belief in racial superiority, and state control of industry.

[11] totalitarianism—government control over every aspect of public and private life.

[12] Kosovo—region in southern Yugoslavia that was the scene of a NATO peace-keeping action in 1999 after Serbian forces murdered large numbers of Albanian civilians living there. The Serbs are the dominant group in Yugoslavia, and the Albanians had been fighting for independence from them.

[13] **covert**—secret.

We will starve terrorists of funding, turn them one against another, drive them from place to place, until there is no refuge or no rest. And we will pursue nations that provide aid or safe haven to terrorism. Every nation, in every region, now has a decision to make. Either you are with us, or you are with the terrorists. From this day forward, any nation that continues to harbor or support terrorism will be regarded by the United States as a hostile regime.

Our nation has been put on notice: We are not immune from attack. We will take defensive measures against terrorism to protect Americans. Today, dozens of federal departments and agencies, as well as state and local governments, have responsibilities affecting homeland security. These efforts must be coordinated at the highest level.

These measures are essential. But the only way to defeat terrorism as a threat to our way of life is to stop it, eliminate it, and destroy it where it grows.

Many will be involved in this effort, from FBI agents to intelligence operatives to the reservists we have called to active duty. All deserve our thanks, and all have our prayers. And tonight, a few miles from the damaged Pentagon, I have a message for our military: Be ready. I've called the Armed Forces to alert, and there is a reason. The hour is coming when America will act, and you will make us proud.

This is not, however, just America's fight. And what is at stake is not just America's freedom. This is the world's fight. This is civilization's fight. This is the fight of all who believe in progress and pluralism, tolerance and freedom.

We ask every nation to join us. We will ask, and we will need, the help of police forces, intelligence services, and banking systems around the world. The United States is grateful that many nations and many international organizations have already responded—with sympathy and with support. Nations from Latin America, to Asia, to Africa, to Europe, to the Islamic world. Perhaps the NATO[14] Charter reflects best the attitude of the world: An attack on one is an attack on all.

The civilized world is rallying to America's side. They understand that if this terror goes unpunished, their own cities, their own citizens may be next. Terror, unanswered, cannot only bring down buildings, it can threaten the stability of legitimate governments. And you know what—we're not going to allow it.

Americans are asking: What is expected of us? I ask you to live your lives, and hug your children. I know many citizens have fears tonight, and I ask you to be calm and resolute, even in the face of a continuing threat.

I ask you to uphold the values of America, and remember why so many have come here. We are in a fight for our principles, and our first responsibility is to live by them. No one should be singled out for unfair treatment or unkind words because of their ethnic background or religious faith.

I ask you to continue to support the victims of this tragedy with your contributions. . . .

I ask for your patience, with the delays and inconveniences that may accompany tighter security; and for your patience in what will be a long struggle.

I ask your continued participation and confidence in the American economy. Terrorists attacked a symbol of American prosperity. They did not touch its source. America is successful because of the hard work, and creativity, and enterprise of our people. These were the true strengths of our economy before September 11th, and they are our strengths today.

And, finally, please continue praying for the victims of terror and their families, for those in uniform, and for

---

[14] NATO—North Atlantic Treaty Organization, a defensive military alliance formed in 1949 by ten Western European nations, the United States, and Canada.

our great country. Prayer has comforted us in sorrow, and will help strengthen us for the journey ahead.

After all that has just passed—all the lives taken, and all the possibilities and hopes that died with them—it is natural to wonder if America's future is one of fear. Some speak of an age of terror. I know there are struggles ahead, and dangers to face. But this country will define our times, not be defined by them. As long as the United States of America is determined and strong, this will not be an age of terror; this will be an age of liberty, here and across the world.

Great harm has been done to us. We have suffered great loss. And in our grief and anger we have found our mission and our moment. Freedom and fear are at war. The advance of human freedom—the great achievement of our time, and the great hope of every time—now depends on us. Our nation—this generation—will lift a dark threat of violence from our people and our future. We will rally the world to this cause by our efforts, by our courage. We will not tire, we will not falter, and we will not fail.

It is my hope that in the months and years ahead, life will return almost to normal. We'll go back to our lives and routines, and that is good. Even grief recedes with time and grace. But our resolve must not pass. Each of us will remember what happened that day, and to whom it happened. We'll remember the moment the news came—where we were and what we were doing. Some will remember an image of a fire, or a story of rescue. Some will carry memories of a face and a voice gone forever.

And I will carry this: It is the police shield of a man named George Howard, who died at the World Trade Center trying to save others. It was given to me by his mom, Arlene, as a proud memorial to her son. This is my reminder of lives that ended, and a task that does not end.

I will not forget this wound to our country or those who inflicted it. I will not yield; I will not rest; I will not relent in waging this struggle for freedom and security for the American people.

The course of this conflict is not known, yet its outcome is certain. Freedom and fear, justice and cruelty, have always been at war, and we know that God is not neutral between them.

Fellow citizens, we'll meet violence with patient justice—assured of the rightness of our cause, and confident of the victories to come. In all that lies before us, may God grant us wisdom, and may He watch over the United States of America.

QUESTIONS TO CONSIDER

1. How does President Bush convey the idea that the terrorist attacks were in a sense a worldwide tragedy, not just an American one?

2. Why is President Bush careful to make distinctions in his address—between Arabs or Muslims and terrorists, and between the people of Afghanistan and the ruling Taliban government?

3. How is the war against terrorism compared to other wars in American history?

4. What does the president mean when he talks about the terrorists' desire to end Americans' "way of life"? What other groups in history does he say were also opposed to American values?

5. The president opens and closes his address by remembering two heroes of September 11. Who are they, and why do you think President Bush does this?

Osama bin Laden on the Attacks

In his address to the nation on September 20, President Bush charged Osama bin Laden and his extremist al-Qaeda organization with responsibility for the September 11 attacks. Many people— particularly in the Islamic world—were skeptical and asked for proof of bin Laden's guilt. In mid-November, a videotape was found in a house in the Afghan city of Jalalabad, when U.S.-backed Afghan forces took the city from the Taliban. It showed bin Laden discussing the attacks with his supporters, and it appeared that those present knew they were being taped. The U.S. Defense Department released the tape along with an English translation that had been made by two independent scholars of Arabic. The following portions of the translation present two conversations between bin Laden, a Shaykh[1] (later identified as a crippled Saudi who had fought in Afghanistan, Bosnia, and Chechnya), and other supporters. Some portions of conversations were impossible to hear, and these are identified as "inaudible." As you read the conversations, remember that the interpretation of Islam expressed here is that of violent extremists.

---

[1] *Shaykh*—often *sheikh*, title for an Islamic religious official.

Shaykh: [*inaudible portion*] You have given us weapons, you have given us hope and we thank Allah for you. We don't want to take much of your time, but this is the arrangement of the brothers. People now are supporting us more, even those ones who did not support us in the past, support us more now. I did not want to take that much of your time. We praise Allah, we praise Allah. We came from Kabul.[2] We were very pleased to visit. May Allah bless you both at home and the camp. We asked the driver to take us, it was a night with a full moon, thanks be to Allah. Believe me it is not in the countryside. The elderly—everybody praises what you did, the great action you did, which was first and foremost by the grace of Allah. This is the guidance of Allah and the blessed fruit of jihad.

bin Laden: Thanks to Allah. What is the stand of the Mosques[3] there (in Saudi Arabia)?

Shaykh: Honestly, they are very positive. Shaykh Al-Bahrani gave a good sermon in his class after the sunset prayers. It was videotaped and I was supposed to carry it with me, but unfortunately, I had to leave immediately.

bin Laden: The day of the events?[4]

Shaykh: At the exact time of the attack on America, precisely at the time, he (Bahrani) gave a very impressive sermon. Thanks be to Allah for his blessings. He (Bahrani) was the first one to write at war time. I visited him twice in Al-Qasim.[5]

bin Laden: Thanks be to Allah.

Shaykh: This is what I asked from Allah. He (Bahrani) told the youth: "You are asking for martyrdom and wonder where you should go (for martyrdom)." Allah was inciting them to go. I asked Allah to grant me

---

[2] Kabul—capital of Afghanistan.

[3] Mosques—Islamic houses of worship. Bin Laden is asking how the Islamic leadership is reacting to the news of the attacks.

[4] events—September 11 attacks.

[5] Al-Qasim—city in Saudi Arabia.

to witness the truth in front of the unjust ruler. We ask Allah to protect him and give him the martyrdom, after he issued the first fatwa. He was detained for interrogation, as you know. When he was called in and asked to sign, he told them, "Don't waste my time, I have another fatwa. If you want me, I can sign both at the same time."

bin Laden: Thanks be to Allah.

Shaykh: His position is really very encouraging. When I paid him the first visit about a year and half ago, he asked me, "How is Shaykh bin-Laden?" He sends you his special regards. As far as Shaykh Sulayman Ulwan is concerned, he gave a beautiful fatwa, may Allah bless him. Miraculously, I heard it on the Quran radio station. It was strange because he (Ulwan) sacrificed his position, which is equivalent to a director. It was transcribed word-by-word. The brothers listened to it in detail. I briefly heard it before the noon prayers. He (Ulwan) said this was jihad and those people were not innocent people (World Trade Center and Pentagon victims). He swore to Allah. This was transmitted to Shaykh Sulayman Al Umar. Allah bless him.

bin Laden: What about Shaykh Al-Rayan?

Shaykh: Honestly, I did not meet with him. My movements were truly limited.

bin Laden: Allah bless you. You are welcome.

Shaykh [*describing the trip to the meeting*]: They smuggled us, and then I thought that we would be in different caves inside the mountains so I was surprised at the guest house and that it is very clean and comfortable. Thanks be to Allah, we also learned that this location is safe, by Allah's blessings. The place is clean and we are very comfortable.

bin Laden: [*inaudible portion*] when people see a strong horse and a weak horse, by nature, they will like the strong horse. This is only one goal; those who want people to worship the lord of the people, without following that doctrine, will be following the doctrine of Muhammad, peace be upon him. [*bin Laden quotes several short and incomplete Hadith[6] verses, as follows*]: "I was ordered to fight the people until they say there is no God but Allah, and his prophet Muhammad." "Some people may ask: why do you want to fight us?" "There is an association between those who say: I believe in one God and Muhammad is his prophet, and those who don't" [*inaudible portion*] "Those who do not follow the true fiqh.[7] The fiqh of Muhammad, the real fiqh. They are just accepting what is being said at face value."

Those youths who conducted the operations did not accept any fiqh in the popular terms, but they accepted the fiqh that the prophet Muhammad brought. Those young men [*inaudible portion*] said in deeds, in New York and Washington, speeches that overshadowed all other speeches made everywhere else in the world. The speeches are understood by both Arabs and non-Arabs—even by Chinese. It is above all the media said. Some of them said that in Holland, at one of the centers, the number of people who accepted Islam during the days that followed the operations were more than the people who accepted Islam in the last eleven years. I heard someone on Islamic radio who owns a school in America say: "We don't have time to keep up with the demands of those who are asking about Islamic books to learn about Islam." This event made people think (about true Islam) which benefited Islam greatly.

Shaykh: Hundreds of people used to doubt you and few only would follow you, until this huge event happened. Now hundreds of people are coming out to join you. I remember a vision by Shaykh Salih Al-Shuaybi. He said: "There will be a great hit, and people will go out by hundreds to Afghanistan." I asked him

---

[6] *Hadith*—Islamic traditions of the sayings and deeds of Muhammad. Muslims revere the Hadith as a sacred text second only to the Quran.

[7] fiqh—Islamic law.

(Salih): "To Afghanistan?" He replied, "Yes." According to him, the only ones who stay behind will be the mentally **impotent**[8] and the liars (hypocrites). I remembered his saying that hundreds of people will go out to Afghanistan. He had this vision a year ago. This event discriminated between the different types of followers.

bin Laden: [*inaudible portion*] we calculated in advance the number of casualties from the enemy, who would be killed based on the position of the tower. We calculated that the floors that would be hit would be three or four floors. I was the most optimistic of them all. [*inaudible portion*] due to my experience in this field, I was thinking that the fire from the gas in the plane would melt the iron structure of the building and collapse the area where the plane hit and all the floors above it only. This is all that we had hoped for.

Shaykh: Allah be praised.

bin Laden: We were at [*inaudible portion*] when the event took place. We had notification since the previous Thursday that the event would take place that day. We had finished our work that day and had the radio on. It was 5:30 P.M. our time. I was sitting with Dr. Ahmad Abu-al-Khair. Immediately, we heard the news that a plane had hit the World Trade Center. We turned the radio station to the news from Washington. The news continued and no mention of the attack until the end. At the end of the newscast, they reported that a plane just hit the World Trade Center.

Shaykh: Allah be praised.

bin Laden: After a little while, they announced that another plane had hit the World Trade Center. The brothers who heard the news were overjoyed by it.

Shaykh: I listened to the news and I was sitting. We didn't—we were not thinking about anything—and all

---

[8] **impotent**—weak.

of a sudden, Allah willing, we were talking about how come we didn't have anything, and all of a sudden the news came and everyone was overjoyed and everyone until the next day, in the morning, was talking about what was happening and we stayed until four o'clock, listening to the news every time a little bit different. Everyone was very joyous and saying "Allah is great," "Allah is great," "We are thankful to Allah," "Praise Allah." And I was happy for the happiness of my brothers. That day the congratulations were coming on the phone non-stop. The mother[9] was receiving phone calls continuously. Thank Allah. Allah is great, praise be to Allah.

[*quoting from the Quran*] "Fight them, Allah will torture them, with your hands, he will torture them. He will deceive them and he will give you victory. Allah will forgive the believers, he is knowledgeable about everything."

No doubt it is a clear victory. Allah has bestowed on us . . . honor on us . . . and he will give us blessing and more victory during this holy month of Ramadan.[10] And this is what everyone is hoping for. Thank Allah, America came out of its caves. We hit her the first hit, and the next one will hit her with the hands of the believers, the good believers, the strong believers. By Allah it is a great work. Allah prepares for you a great reward for this work. I'm sorry to speak in your presence, but it is just thoughts, just thoughts. By Allah, who there is no god but him. I live in happiness, happiness— I have not experienced, or felt, in a long time.

I remember, the words of Al-Rabbani,[11] he said they made a **coalition**[12] against us in the winter with the

---

[9] mother—presumably, the mother of one of those involved in the September 11 attacks.

[10] Ramadan—Islamic month of fasting.

[11] Al-Rabbani—one of several possible Islamic scholars.

[12] **coalition**—alliance.

infidels[13] like the Turks, and others, and some other Arabs. And they surrounded us like the days—in the days of the prophet Muhammad. Exactly like what's happening right now. But he comforted his followers and said, "This is going to turn and hit them back." And it is a mercy for us. And a blessing to us. And it will bring people back. Look how wise he was. And Allah will give him blessing. And the day will come when the symbols of Islam will rise up and it will be similar to the early days of Al-Mujahedeen and Al-Ansar[14] (similar to the early years of Islam). And victory to those who follow Allah. Finally said, if it is the same, like the old days, such as Abu Bakr and Othman and Ali[15] and others. In these days, in our times, that it will be the greatest jihad in the history of Islam and the resistance of the wicked people.

By Allah my Shaykh, we congratulate you for the great work. Thank Allah.

*   *   *

bin Laden: Abdallah Azzam, Allah bless his soul, told me not to record anything [*inaudible portion*] so I thought that was a good omen, and Allah will bless us [*inaudible portion*]. Abu-Al-Hasan Al-Masri, who appeared on Al-Jazeera TV[16] a couple of days ago and addressed the Americans saying: "If you are true men, come down here and face us." [*inaudible portion*] He told me a year ago: "I saw in a dream, we were playing a soccer game against the Americans. When our team showed up in the field, they were all pilots!" He said:

---

[13] **infidels**—unbelievers; here, non-Muslims.

[14] Al-Mujahedeen and Al-Ansar—early Islamic fighters and martyrs regarded as models of piety.

[15] Abu Bakr and Othman and Ali—first three caliphs, or successors of Muhammad, who governed Islam in the mid-600s.

[16] Al-Jazeera TV— Arab satellite TV channel, the only station with cameras in Afghanistan in the days following the September 11 attacks.

"So I wondered if that was a soccer game or a pilot game? Our players were pilots." He (Abu-Al-Hasan) didn't know anything about the operation until he heard it on the radio. He said the game went on and we defeated them. That was a good omen for us.

Shaykh: May Allah be blessed.

Unidentified Man Off-camera: Abd Al Rahman Al-Ghamri said he saw a vision, before the operation, a plane crashed into a tall building. He knew nothing about it.

Shaykh: May Allah be blessed!

Sulayman Abu Guaith: I was sitting with the Shaykh in a room, then I left to go to another room where there was a TV set. The TV broadcasted the big event. The scene was showing an Egyptian family sitting in their living room, they exploded with joy. Do you know when there is a soccer game and your team wins, it was the same expression of joy. There was a subtitle that read: "In revenge for the children of Al Aqsa,[17] Osama bin Laden executes an operation against America." So I went back to the Shaykh (meaning bin Laden) who was sitting in a room with 50 to 60 people. I tried to tell him about what I saw, but he made gesture with his hands, meaning: "I know, I know . . . "

bin Laden: He did not know about the operation. Not everybody knew [*inaudible portion*]. Mohamed Atta[18] from the Egyptian family (meaning the al-Qaeda Egyptian group), was in charge of the group.

Shaykh: A plane crashing into a tall building was out of anyone's imagination. This was a great job. He was one of the pious men in the organization. He became a martyr. Allah bless his soul.

---

[17] children of Al Aqsa—Palestinian children killed in the conflict that began in September 2000 between Israel and the Palestinians; called the "Al-Aqsa Intifada" to distinguish from an earlier intifada (Arabic, "uprising").

[18] Mohamed Atta—one of the leaders of the September 11 attacks. See page 140.

Shaykh [*referring to dreams and visions*]: The plane that he saw crashing into the building was seen before by more than one person. One of the good religious people has left everything and come here. He told me, "I saw a vision, I was in a huge plane, long and wide. I was carrying it on my shoulders and I walked from the road to the desert for half a kilometer. I was dragging the plane." I listened to him and I prayed to Allah to help him. Another person told me that last year he saw, but I didn't understand and I told him I don't understand. He said, "I saw people who left for jihad . . . and they found themselves in New York . . . in Washington and New York." I said, "What is this?" He told me the plane hit the building. That was last year. We haven't thought much about it. But, when the incidents happened he came to me and said, "Did you see . . . this is strange." I have another man . . . my God . . . he said and swore by Allah that his wife had seen the incident a week earlier. She saw the plane crashing into a building . . . that was unbelievable, my God.

bin Laden: The brothers who conducted the operation—all they knew was that they have a martyrdom operation, and we asked each of them to go to America. But they didn't know anything about the operation, not even one letter. But they were trained, and we did not reveal the operation to them until they are there and just before they boarded the planes.

[*inaudible portion*] then he said: Those who were trained to fly didn't know the others. One group of people did not know the other group. [*inaudible portion*] [*Someone in the crowd asks bin Laden to tell the Shaykh about the dream of Abu-Da'ud.*]

We were at a camp of one of the brother's guards in Kandahar. This brother belonged to the majority of the group. He came close and told me that he saw, in a dream, a tall building in America, and in the same dream he saw Mukhtar[19] teaching them how to play karate. At that point, I was worried that maybe the secret would be revealed if everyone starts seeing it in their dream. So I closed the subject. I told him if he sees another dream, not to tell anybody, because people will be upset with him. [*Another person's voice can be heard recounting his dream about two planes hitting a big building.*]

bin Laden: They were overjoyed when the first plane hit the building, so I said to them: be patient. The difference between the first and the second plane hitting the towers was twenty minutes. And the difference between the first plane and the plane that hit the Pentagon was one hour.

Shaykh: They (the Americans) were terrified thinking there was a **coup**.[20]

bin Laden [*reciting a poem*]: "I witness that against the sharp blade they always faced difficulties and stood together. When the darkness comes upon us and we are bit by a sharp tooth, I say 'Our homes are flooded with blood and the tyrant is freely wandering in our homes.' And from the battlefield vanished the brightness of swords and the horses. And over weeping sounds now we hear the beats of drums and rhythm. They are storming his forts and shouting: 'We will not stop our raids until you free our lands.'"

---

[19] Mukhtar—"the Chosen One," an Islamic title usually referring to Muhammad.

[20] **coup**—violent overthrow of a government.

QUESTIONS TO CONSIDER

1. What effect did bin Laden and the Shaykh feel the September 11 attacks was having on Islam?

2. What effect did the Shaykh feel the attacks had had on bin Laden's position as a leader?

3. What did bin Laden mean when he said that those who carried out the attacks "said in deeds, in New York and Washington, speeches that overshadowed all other speeches made everywhere else in the world"?

4. How much destruction did bin Laden and his supporters expect to result from their attack on the World Trade Center?

5. Why do you think that the aftermath of the attacks reminded the Shaykh of the early days of Islam?

6. How much did most of those who carried out the attacks know in advance about the operation?

September 11, 2001

▲
People run down Broadway as a smoke and dust cloud comes up the street
from the collapsing World Trade Center buildings in New York.

◀ Both World Trade Center towers are ablaze after two hijacked airliners
crashed into them.

▲
A section of the Pentagon in Washington, D.C., is destroyed when a hijacked airliner crashes into the building.

◄ Firefighters raise an American flag over the rubble of the World Trade Center.

Firefighters work near the base of the destroyed World Trade Center towers. ▶

▲
Families of missing persons post pictures of their loved ones around New York City after the World Trade Center attack.

◄ Firefighters, police, and rescue workers sift through the rubble of the World Trade Center searching for victims. No survivors were found after the first 24 hours.

◀ U.S. Federal investigators search for clues near the damaged area of the Pentagon.

The FBI unveils a new most-wanted list on October 10, 2001, following the September 11 attacks.
▼

▲

This note was on a bouquet left in front of the U.S. embassy in Sarajevo, the capital of Bosnia-Herzegovina, three days after the attacks. It reads, "You helped us when it was the most difficult for us. With all our hearts we are with you and your children in this terrible sorrow and pain."

A girl wrapped in a U.S. flag watches a funeral procession for a firefighter killed in the World Trade Center attack. ▶

Examining Terrorism

What Is Terrorism?

Terrorism is notoriously difficult to define. The historian Walter Laqueur wrote that "Terrorism is violence, but not every form of violence is terrorism. It is . . . not a synonym for civil war, banditry, or guerrilla warfare." The FBI defines terrorism as the "unlawful use of force or violence against persons or property to intimidate or coerce a government, the civilian population, or any segment thereof, in furtherance of political or social objectives." This could be a definition of guerrilla warfare under many circumstances. There is a saying that "One man's terrorist is another man's freedom fighter." This means that what is defined as terrorism has more to do with point of view than actual events. One thing that does distinguish terrorism from most other types of warfare is that it targets ordinary people rather than the government or military of a nation. An excerpt from a speech given in 1984 by George Schultz, the U.S. Secretary of State under Ronald Reagan, and a 1996 article from The Economist magazine consider what qualifies as terrorism.

The Anatomy of Terrorism

by George Schultz

Let me speak briefly about the anatomy of terrorism. What we have learned about terrorism, first of all, is that it is not random, undirected, purposeless violence. It is not, like an earthquake or a hurricane, an act of nature before which we are helpless. Terrorists and those who support them have definite goals; terrorist violence is the means of attaining those goals. Our response must be twofold: we must deny them the means but above all we must deny them their goals.

But what are the goals of terrorism? We know that the phenomenon of terrorism is actually a matrix that covers a diverse array of methods, resources, instruments, and immediate aims. It appears in many shapes and sizes—from the lone individual who plants a home-made explosive in a shopping center, to the small **clandestine**[1] group that plans kidnappings and assassinations of public figures, to the well-equipped and well-financed organization that uses force to terrorize an entire population. Its stated objectives may range from **separatist**[2] causes to revenge for ethnic grievances to social and political revolution. International drug smugglers use terrorism to blackmail and intimidate government officials. It is clear that our responses will have to fit the precise character and circumstances of the specific threats.

But we must understand that the overarching goal of all terrorists is the same: with rare exceptions, they are attempting to impose their will by force—a special kind of force designed to create an atmosphere of fear. And their efforts are directed at destroying what all of us here are seeking to build. They're a threat to the democracies.

---

[1] **clandestine**—kept or done in secret, often in order to conceal an illicit or improper purpose.

[2] **separatist**—one who advocates cultural, ethnic, religious, or racial separation, especially from a larger group or political unit.

The Use of Terror

from *The Economist*

JUNE 1914: A young man in Sarajevo steps up to a carriage and fires his pistol. Archduke Ferdinand dies. Within weeks, the first world war has begun. The 1940s: the French resistance kill occupying troops when and how they can. June 1944: at Oradour-sur-Glane, in central France, German SS troops take revenge, massacring 642 villagers. August 1945: the United States Air Force drops the world's first nuclear weapons. Some 190,000 Japanese die, nearly all of them civilians. Within days the second world war has ended.

Which of these four events was an act of terrorism? Which achieved anything? Which, if any, will history judge as justified? And whose history? Terrorism is not the simple, sharp-edged, bad-guy phenomenon we all love to condemn. No clear line marks off politics from the threat of force, threat from use, use from covert or open war. Who is or is not a terrorist? The suicide bomber, the rebel guerrilla, the liberation front, the armed forces of the state?

In practice, what act or person earns the label depends on who wants to apply it. To Ulster loyalists[3] all IRA violence is terrorism; to Sinn Fein[4] it is part of a legitimate war. To many Israelis, everyone from the suicide-bombers in Jerusalem or Ashkelon to the Hezbollah[5] grenade-thrower in South Lebanon is a terrorist; to many Arabs during the 1982 Lebanon war,

---

[3] Ulster loyalists—those in Northern Ireland (or Ulster) who want it to remain part of Great Britain.

[4] Sinn Fein—Gaelic, "Ourselves Alone" or "We Ourselves," political arm of the Irish Republican Army, an organization whose goal is to add British-controlled Northern Ireland to the independent Republic of Ireland by any means necessary.

[5] Hezbollah—Arabic, "The Party of God," a Shiite Muslim guerrilla movement based in Lebanon and backed by Iran.

the worst terrorists in the Middle East were the—entirely legitimate, uniformed—Israel Defense Force.

If the concept is not to vanish into all-embracing fudge, two distinctions can be drawn, though habitually they are not. Terrorism is indeed about terror; not just violence, but its use to spread terror. And the violence is aimed specifically at civilians.

Classical terrorism, ideological rather than territorial, reveals the **niceties**.[6] Recent decades saw West Germany's Baader-Meinhof gang and Red Army Faction murder prominent businessmen such as Alfred Herrhausen and Jurgen Ponto (bosses of Germany's two largest banks, Deutsche and Dresdner respectively). Italy's Red Brigades murdered Aldo Moro, a former prime minister. Its far right in 1980 blew up a train in Bologna station, killing 84 people. Which of these was truly terrorism? Arguably, only the last. It was an act of indiscriminate violence to terrorize citizens at large; the others were discriminate assassinations to win publicity and display power.

Likewise, lobbing mortar-bombs into a British army base in South Armagh may have deadly results, but it is guerrilla warfare. Planting a bomb that kills a dozen diners in a restaurant is terrorism. The suicide bomber in Jerusalem was a terrorist; the Hezbollah fighter in South Lebanon attacking Israeli army patrols is not.

Even in the distinction between guerrilla warfare and terrorism, there are grey areas. The soldier in a tank is a military target. What about one in a jeep escorting civilian vehicles? Or returning on a bus from leave? A bus that may—and was, when a suicide bomber attacked it in Gaza[7] last April—be carrying civilians too?

---

[6] **niceties**—fine distinctions.

[7] Gaza—city in the Gaza Strip, a narrow coastal area along the Mediterranean Sea adjoining Israel and Egypt. Gaza was under Israeli military rule until 1994, when a phased transfer of authority to Palestinians began.

There are, in contrast, distinctions often made that ought not to be. What is or is not "terrorism" does not depend on the badness or goodness of the cause, nor on whether those espousing it have the chance to express their demands democratically. When President James Garfield was assassinated in America in the same year, 1881, that a Russian terrorist group blew up Tsar Alexander II, the Russians wrote an open letter condemning Garfield's killers and arguing that:

> In a land where the citizens are free to express their ideas, and where the will of the people does not merely make the law but appoints the person who is to carry the law into effect, political assassination is the manifestation of despotism. . . . Despotism is always blameworthy and force can only be justified when employed to resist force.

Yet despotism does not justify throwing bombs into crowds (as the group sometimes did).

The fact is that a good cause may use terrorism just as a bad one may. South Africa has provided a clear example. The ending of white dominance was a plainly good cause. For the most part, the African National Congress[8] used mass demonstrations and industrial sabotage to advance its cause. But the men who shot up a white church congregation or planted a bomb outside a cinema were terrorists in the purest sense of the word.

Nor does the terrorists' ultimate success or failure alter the truth. Menachem Begin[9] got to lead a country;

---

[8] African National Congress—organization that led the resistance to South Africa's racial policies.

[9] Menachem Begin—Israeli prime minister in the late 1970s during the historic peace process with Egypt. He had been a leader of the Irgun, a Zionist terror group dedicated to driving the British out of Palestine. See note on page 131.

Yasir Arafat[10] may do; Velupillai Prabhakaran, who leads the Tamil Tigers,[11] probably will not. None of that changes the fact that Deir Yassin (a massacre of Palestinian villagers by Israelis fighting to establish their state), the killing of 11 Israeli athletes at the Munich Olympics in 1972, and this year's Tamil Tiger bomb in Colombo were all acts of terror.

So much for the underdogs. Can there be terrorist governments too? The Americans certainly think so when they accuse Libya or Iran of supporting international terrorism. In the cold war, international terrorists were used to wage war by proxy: the East German regime provided safe houses for Baaders and Meinhofs; the modern era's most notorious terrorist, the gun-for-hire Carlos the Jackal, made his career in this world of state-sponsored terrorism.

All that was diplomacy by terror. Can a recognized government also be guilty of terrorism against its own people?

Yes. Stalin[12] used terror systematically to consolidate his power—random murders of Communist-Party members and army officers in the 1930s, massacres and exiles of smaller ethnic groups throughout his rule. Much of Latin America practiced state terrorism in recent decades. The brass hat regimes[13] of the day faced left-wing, sometimes terrorist movements. Many fought back with terror. And not just through paramilitaries[14] or unacknowledged death squads. The infamous massacre

---

[10] Yasir Arafat—president of the Palestinian Authority, the government of the Palestinian people in areas controlled by Israel. After 1969, he was the leader of the Palestine Liberation Organization (PLO), whose military wing conducted an armed struggle against Israel.

[11] Tamil Tigers—nationalist guerrilla and terrorist organization in Sri Lanka.

[12] Stalin—Joseph Stalin (1879–1953), dictator who ruled the Soviet Union from the late 1920s until his death.

[13] brass hat regimes—military governments.

[14] paramilitaries—groups that are organized and function like military units but not as part of regular military forces.

at El Mozote in El Salvador in 1981 was the work of that country's regular army. The unit that did it had a cheerful song of its own, "Somos Guerreros":

> We are warriors,
> Warriors all!
> We are setting out to kill
> A mountain of terrorists.

What in fact they killed was over 500 peasants; probably the worst "official" massacre in Latin America's recent history.

Can regular armies, in regular war, be guilty of terrorism? The answer, surely, is yes. Look at the Japanese rape of Nanking in 1937, when not hundreds or thousands but tens of thousands of civilians were murdered, to terrorize the rest of China. Then go a step further. Can the armies of proud democracies be guilty too? A century ago, the rich world, with the rules of war that it claimed to use, would have called attacking civilians impermissible. The modern world has other ideas. The Allied[15] bombing of Germany was aimed at civilians in the hope of shattering morale: in short, terror. The fire bombing of Tokyo and the atomic weapons that vaporized Hiroshima and Nagasaki were arguably aimed at government morale, not that of Japan's population. Their victims did not notice the difference.

What use, one can ask, is a definition so wide that it can go from Stalin to the American air force? There are two answers.

First, it is a reminder that terrorism, historically, has been the tool of the strong, not the weak. Medieval armies, having taken a besieged town, would slaughter some or all of the citizens to encourage other towns to

---

[15] Allied—from Allied Powers, also called the Allies; the countries that fought against the Axis Powers (Germany, Italy, and Japan) in World War II. The Allies included Great Britain, France, the Soviet Union, the United States, and China.

surrender faster. During India's struggle for independence, by far the worst terror was the Amritsar massacre in 1919, when British-officered troops shot up a political gathering, and carried on shooting until the bullets ran out; 379 civilians died (and it worked: the rebellious province of Punjab returned to order). In contrast, discriminate assassination was the typical weapon of the 19th-century anarchist and nihilist.[16]

By and large, true random terrorism has come in the past 30 years, as in the Bologna train bomb, the recent nerve-gassing of the Tokyo metro by a religious cult, or the Oklahoma City bomb; all three crimes were aimed at no matter whom for a purpose so vague or Utopian as to seem irrelevant, except to the deranged. Even in this period most—not all—IRA killing was aimed at defined targets: soldiers, policemen, individual Protestant farmers in border areas. The Basque violence of ETA[17] has often followed this pattern. Peru's Shining Path guerrillas are truer terrorists, but even they (mostly) prefer the tactics, honed by the Vietcong,[18] of killing officials, not just (as in some infamous massacres) everyone in sight. Algeria's and Sri Lanka's terrorists today probably have the strongest claim to be called spreaders of true random terror.

The second thing one can learn from the wide definition is that the phenomenon is neither uniquely wicked, nor—still less—uniquely deadly. People fight with the weapons they have: knives, Semtex,[19] rifles,

---

[16] anarchist and nihilist—Anarchism and nihilism were two radical, anti-government political movements that began in the 19th century.

[17] Basque ... ETA—Basques are a people who live in the area that overlaps the border of Spain with France. The ETA is an offshoot of the Basque Nationalist Party; it began in 1959 out of frustration at not being able to use armed struggle. Since then, the ETA has used such terrorist methods as bombing and assassination in its campaign to create a Basque state independent of Spain.

[18] Vietcong—group of communist guerrillas in South Vietnam who, with the help of North Vietnam, fought against the South Vietnamese government in the Vietnam War (1954–1975).

[19] Semtex—explosive that is popular with terrorists.

fighter-bombers. All their users are alike convinced of their own righteousness, all kill and all their victims are equally dead. What they are not is equal in number. The Munich terrorists killed 11 Israelis; Israel's retaliation against the Lebanese town of Nabatiyeh, however justified, killed about 100 Arabs. The State Department has totted up the deaths due to international terrorism from 1968 through 1995. Its total, and it defines terrorism broadly, is 8,700. Twenty-four hours of air raids killed six times as many in Dresden in 1945. One is a crime, says international law, the other a legitimate act of war.

QUESTIONS TO CONSIDER

1. According to George Schultz, what is the main goal of terrorism?

2. Schultz suggests that government responses to terrorism must "fit the precise character . . . of the specific threats." What is your opinion of this view?

3. What does Schultz mean when he says that terrorists want to destroy "what all of us . . . are seeking to build"?

4. What is meant in *The Economist* article by the statement, "Terrorism is not the simple, sharp-edged, bad-guy phenomenon we all love to condemn"?

5. How does the article define *terrorism*? What is your opinion of this definition?

6. Why is it important how governments define *terrorism*?

Who Is a Terrorist?

INTERVIEW WITH BRIAN JENKINS

What defines most terrorists is their goals. The majority of terrorist organizations are nationalist. The IRA wants a united Ireland; much of the anti-Israel terrorism is aimed at the creation of a Palestinian state; the Tamil Tigers want an independent homeland in Sri Lanka. A second major category of terrorists is those whose goals are communist or anti-capitalist. In the 1970's, the Red Brigades and the Baader-Meinhof Gang wanted to hasten a communist revolution in Europe. A third kind of terrorist is motivated by religion; some of the Islamic terrorist groups aim to topple their country's secular regimes and replace them with fundamentalist rule. Osama bin Laden's al-Qaeda movement is religious in character. What unites most terrorists is their desire for attention. Brian Jenkins, a terrorism expert, wrote in the 1970s: "Terrorists want a lot of people watching and a lot of people listening and not a lot of people dead." In a 1994 interview in Omni *magazine, Jenkins tries to define who is a terrorist.*

Omni: Who is a terrorist?

Jenkins: Not the serial killer, the driveby shooter; not the employee who gets fired and returns to the post office with an assault rifle. Terrorism is not irrational violence. Not that terrorists think as you or I, but they have their own terrible logic. Their actions are calculated to create an atmosphere of fear and alarm to force social or political change. We have laws against the things terrorists do—murder, kidnapping, arson. They sometimes claim to be above these laws as soldiers at war. Yasir Arafat once said that no one who stands for a just cause is a terrorist. But we do not define a terrorist by his cause; we know him by the quality of his act.

Omni: The World Trade Center bombing was on the anniversary date of our first air attack of Desert Storm.[1] One analyst said it shows the Gulf War is still on—for Muslims.

Jenkins: At Rand, we were once asked to find all dates of significance to various groups. Well, the calendar is completely filled. I can guarantee you a bomb will go off somewhere in Latin America on July 26, the anniversary of the Cuban Revolution, like a greeting card. I doubt the date of the Trade Center bombings had any magical meaning. What brought them together and gave them a sense of mission were their religious views, their support of Muslims fighting the Soviets in Afghanistan, and the trial of their comrade El Sayyid Nosair for the murder of Rabbi Meir Kahane.[2]

Immigrating to a vastly different culture, they also faced prejudice, derision, isolation. They reacted by hurtling themselves into religious-political fervency. What must it be like for a devout Muslim to come to a city like New York? One is regularly insulted just for being there. Abouhalima[3] drove a cab, with cars cutting him off, people shouting obscenities. They saw nudity

---

[1] World Trade Center bombing . . . Desert Storm—The interviewer is referring to the first attack on the World Trade Center in 1993. Desert Storm was the U.S.-led military operation of the Persian Gulf War.

[2] Meir Kahane—Jewish political extremist who pushed for the removal of all Arabs from Israel, by violence if necessary.

[3] Abouhalima—one of those involved in the 1993 World Trade Center bombing.

on billboards, rampant materialism.[4] To someone with their beliefs, such images and attitudes daily mocked their religion and culture. They wanted to strike out against a society they loathed.

Omni: How is the immigrant transformed into a terrorist?

Jenkins: Terrorism begins with a conspiracy. And a conspiracy begins as talk. "How did these clowns become the government?" "I can't stand the **depravity**[5] of this society." Conversations are **fervent**;[6] you slam your fist on the table. You burn with rage. You decide you're willing to go beyond talk and do something. But you'll need help. A bit of testing goes on. Maybe you and I held protest signs at Nosair's trial or prayed at the same mosque or trained together to fight in Afghanistan. This gives you confidence I won't call the cops. You take me aside and say, "We must do something." Now we are sliding into conspiracy. I say, "My cousin will come in on this." You say, "So will my good friend." And it begins to grow. It is an intimate and fragile thing. Maybe one person in your circle leaves the room whenever there is talk of taking action. He will be assessed as someone to leave out of the conspiracy. Maybe whenever you say, "Something must be done," Abdul shouts, "All of them should be blown up!" Ah, there's someone to approach.

This is a self-selecting group of angry, action-oriented people. Most core members are true believers. Then others come in for membership itself. Like in street gangs or an army unit, people join to participate, to wear the colors. Their ideological grounding may be lower than the founders', but their dedication to violence may be higher. It's what the group does—the violence—that

---

[4] rampant materialism—widespread concern with possessions.

[5] **depravity**—moral corruption.

[6] **fervent**—full of emotion.

attracts them. Finally the psychopaths, the thugs, join. For them terrorism satisfies emotional needs. It is a license to blow things up, to kill. Their dedication to ideology is very low; their dedication to violence, high. The thugs begin to dominate decision-making. Fearing labels like "soft" or " traitor," the leaders are virtually blackmailed into escalating violence. As founder of a self-selected extremist group, how can you retain control if you are seen as less extreme than the most extreme?

Omni: The authorities cited the "witches brew" at the World Trade Center as evidence of their amateurism.

Jenkins: That was just dangerous chemistry. They could have blown themselves up on the highway in New Jersey. Years ago someone published the Anarchist Cookbook that gave a recipe for making nitroglycerin on your kitchen stove. I half-suspected the authorities put it out to eliminate people crazy enough to try it. They left fingerprints, took no internal security precautions, used their real names when renting the van. Found in their possession were not only manuals on bomb making, but books about knives and martial arts.

I've seen this peculiar fascination with all instruments of violence before. Hostages from terrorist kidnappings have told me their captors would get out of bed, disassemble their weapons, clean, and oil them. In the afternoon they'd do it again. They are fascinated by instruments of violence. In one case, kidnappers introduced their hostage to the submachine gun that killed the American ambassador as if it were alive. Terrorists spend a lot of time fondling and talking about weapons. If you bugged their lampshade, you'd think they were up to bombing nuclear plants or kidnapping the Pope. It's mostly pretending. These are amateurs.

Omni: But not harmless.

Jenkins: Extremely dangerous. Inspired by religious fervor, they have a mandate from God to dismiss constraints against using violence. The Trade Center bombers didn't worry about offending their constituency—their constituency was outside this world. This is sanction-of-God stuff in their heads: The deaths were justified and they think it's a shame only six people died.

Omni: A terrorist driven by political cause would not have done this?

Jenkins: A seemingly normal, nice person always comes down after every lecture or briefing I give and says, "If I were a terrorist, I'd . . . " and lays out the most diabolical scheme. Armchair terrorists can conjure up terrible things terrorists in the field have not done. Why? Because most terrorists impose constraints on themselves. Their violence is not an end in itself, but for advancing a goal. Political terrorists, believing they're the vanguard of the people's will, use violence to shock, get publicity, and leverage a government. They know if they act too horribly, they may alienate their perceived constituents, create public backlash, or provoke the police to crack down on them—with popular support. The Irish Republican Army receives political and financial support from people it doesn't want to upset. When I R A members are about to set off a bomb in London, they warn the police so people can get out of the way. Or at least they want to be seen as providing warning.

Omni: Will terrorism become increasingly more deadly?

Jenkins: Probably more large-scale, indiscriminate violence. That's a trend. The first bombings were extraordinary events, but the 400th bombing was just another bombing. Seeking to escalate the shock, terrorists are forced to set off bigger bombs. Governments have defended preferred targets like airports and embassies, so terrorists have moved to softer targets like department stores, public buildings, or crowded streets. The Trade Center incident was but only one of 100 terrorist car bombings in 1993, in Florence, Bogota, Lima, the financial district of London; in Bombay, 300 people died from a car bomb in the street.

The engine that drives armed conflict in the next century will not be ideological quarrels so much as religious and ethnic conflict. Most of the 30 armed conflicts going on now are based on religious or ethnic differences. This type of conflict lends itself to atrocities, the kind of violence seen in the slaughter of women and children in Rwanda,[7] the massacre of Palestinians in prayer at Hebron, the World Trade Center. Through the mouth of a sheik in a Jersey City mosque, God says it is proper to kill infidels. God whispers in the ear of a Jewish fanatic to gun down his enemies. In an ethnic war, your death may be the very purpose of my struggle. If you are not a member of my tribe, I consider you barely human. A goat that gives milk is of more value.

---

[7] Rwanda—nation in east central Africa that in 1994 was the site of massive ethnic violence. Roughly half a million civilians, mostly of the Tutsi people, were killed by rival Hutus. Thousands of Rwandans from both groups became refugees, fleeing into the neighboring country of the Congo, then called Zaire.

QUESTIONS TO CONSIDER

1. Who does Brian Jenkins say a terrorist is *not*?

2. How realistic do you think is Jenkins's description of how a terrorist group might start and grow?

3. Why does Jenkins say that the original leaders of such a group might feel pressure to increase their use of violence?

4. What does Jenkins mean when he says that the constituency of the World Trade Center bombers of 1993 was "outside this world"?

5. In Jenkins's view, why do terrorists impose limits on themselves? What is your opinion of his view?

Terrorism in the Twenty-first Century

BY YONAH ALEXANDER

Many countries are the target of terrorist campaigns: Great Britain by the IRA, Spain by the Basque separatists of the ETA, India by the Kashmiri separatists. All can be characterized in some way as a nationalist struggle against an occupying power; but over the last two decades anti-American terrorism has risen dramatically without such a simple cause. The attacks by suicide bombers on the American embassy and a U.S. Marine barracks in Beirut in 1983 were a wake-up call for the U.S. government, which began actively to fight and try to stop terrorism. These measures had immediate effect, but in the 1990s terrorist activity again began to rise and the violence of the attacks escalated. The 1995 attack in Oklahoma City and the 1998 embassy bombings in Africa saw the United States decisively step up its anti-terrorist activities, as did the September 11 attacks. But the continuing terrorist attacks show how difficult it is for Western governments to stop attacks perpetrated by small, dedicated terror groups. In a 1999 article in The World & I, *terrorism expert Yonah Alexander traced the recent trends in terrorism and pointed out why most experts see terrorism continuing to rise.*

An analysis of global trends in 1998 concluded that subnational and government-sponsored terrorism in the name of "higher principles" was the most intensive in three decades. The costly figures in 1997 (221 dead and 690 wounded) were surpassed on a single day on August 7, 1998, when the nearly simultaneous car bombs at the U.S. embassies in Kenya and Tanzania killed 260 people and injured 5,000 others.

Similarly last year, a powerful bomb in Omagh, Northern Ireland, killed or wounded 250 people in the single worst attack of Ulster's **sectarian**[1] violence. In Israel (as well as the territories and the "security" zone in Lebanon) the casualty cost of civilians and soldiers killed and wounded reached over 500. And scores of other countries around the world—such as Algeria, Colombia, India, Spain, Sri Lanka, Pakistan, and Turkey—have continued to be plagued by deadly terrorist attacks.

This bloody record underscores the point that **anarchy**[2] is becoming a universal nightmare. It is safe to assume, therefore, that terrorism will continue into the twenty-first century. This **prognosis**[3] is based on the fact that many of the issues that motivate terrorists will remain unresolved. Moreover, new issues will develop into expanded political confrontations.

There are several reasons why terrorism will grow in the future. First, it has proved successful in attracting publicity, disrupting government and business activities, and causing significant death and destruction. Second, arms, explosives, supplies, financing, and secret communications are readily available. Third, an international support network of groups and states greatly facilitates the undertaking of terrorist activities.

---

[1] **sectarian**—relating to sects.

[2] **anarchy**—absence of any form of political authority; political disorder and confusion.

[3] **prognosis**—forecast.

Future attacks are sure to be characterized by both continuity and change. Groups that are small and unsophisticated can be expected to rely mostly on bombings. Those with more skills and state support will probably attempt to carry out more complex operations, such as kidnappings, assassinations, and facility attacks.

Moreover, technological developments offer new targets and new capabilities for terrorist groups. Consequently, future incidents could be much more costly in terms of human lives and property, given the availability of biological, chemical, and nuclear weapons.

Although no major incidents involving major destruction have occurred, the historical record of the past three decades provides evidence of terrorist groups' being involved with some type of unconventional operations. In 1972, members of the Order of the Rising Sun in the United States possessed 30–40 kilograms of typhoid[4] bacteria cultures, which they intended to use to infect water supplies in major Midwest cities.

Similarly, in 1974, right-wing Italian terrorists planned to poison their country's water supplies with radioactive uranium stolen from a nuclear center. In 1980, police in Paris discovered a biological laboratory with *clostridium botulinum* culture belonging to the German Baader-Meinhof Gang. In 1986, the Rajneesh religious cult in Oregon used a typhoid *(salmonella typhi)* to contaminate salad bars in restaurants; this resulted in 750 cases of food poisoning.

It was not until March 20, 1995, however, that the first major use of chemical weapons by terrorists took place. Members of the Japanese radical cult Aum Shinrikyo placed containers of the deadly chemical nerve agent Sarin on five trains of the Tokyo subway

---

[4] typhoid—short for typhoid fever, an acute infectious disease caused by the bacteria in contaminated food and water. After about four weeks of high fever, organ damage and other severe complications can occur.

system. The cultists then punctured the containers and released poisonous gas into the trains and subway stations. The attack resulted in the death of 12 persons, and 5,500 others were injured.

In addition to superterrorism—biological, chemical, and nuclear—there is growing apprehension over cyberterrorism. More specifically, concern over the vulnerability of computer networks is sending computer security spending well into the billions—and with good reason. Cyber attacks began to occur over the last few years, and all statistics indicate that they will continue to grow. In 1996, several major financial institutions in London paid large sums of money to gangs of "cyberterrorists," or hackers, who threatened to destroy computer systems. In 1997, the U.S. Department of Energy had its entire system wiped out by the "Trojan horse" virus, a product of cyberterrorism.

Computer security threats can be roughly divided into three general groups: malicious threats, unintentional threats, and physical threats. The first category, malicious threats, covers electronic means for attacking an information system. Hackers, either state-sponsored or working independently, will use computer viruses such as worms, Trojan horses, logic bombs, and electronic bacteria to damage or destroy information.

In short, terrorist abuse of the advances of science and technology is turning all societies into potential victims. As such, there is no immunity for the noncombatant segment or for nations with no direct connection to political violence motivated by particular conflicts. Superterrorism is therefore likely to have an unprecedented, serious impact on the future of civilized existence.

Two factors suggest the likely development of more destructive forms of terrorism well into the twenty-first century. First, increasing security measures and using preemptive and punitive military strikes to control violence might, in fact, hasten the **advent**[5] of more daring types of terrorism. As a result of this trend, other vulnerable targets created by technological advances are likely to become more attractive to terrorists.

Second, terrorism might escalate because violence based on ideology or politics is usually a means to an end: It progresses in proportion to the aims envisioned. If the goals are higher, then the level of terrorism must necessarily be higher. According to intelligence reports, the world's most notorious terrorist, Osama bin Laden, who allegedly masterminded the bombings of the two embassies in East Africa, is attempting to obtain enriched uranium for the purpose of developing nuclear weapons. Hovering in the wings is the threat of "unconventional terror" by state sponsors like Iraq, Iran, Libya, Sudan, and Syria.

The United States is a principal target of terrorism. Not only do domestic extremist groups commit acts of terrorism at home, but international groups attack American targets abroad. However, it should be noted that international acts of terrorism have rarely occurred on U.S. soil.

During the 1970s, **indigenous**[6] and foreign terrorist campaigns in the United States resulted in 600 attacks against civilians and military targets. The success of counterterrorist activities by the FBI and law-enforcement agencies, coupled with changes in the global political environment, reduced the frequency of domestic terrorism in the 1980s. During the last decade, the number of terrorist incidents was 200, a two-thirds decrease from the 1970s.

The 1990s marked an escalation of dramatic incidents of terrorism. The 1993 bombing of the World Trade Center by Middle East subversives killed 6 people and injured more than 1,000 (the plot to destroy New York

---

[5] **advent**—coming.

[6] **indigenous**—native to a region or country.

landmarks was aborted). In 1995, American terrorists with ties to paramilitary forces destroyed a federal building in Oklahoma City, killing 168 and injuring 500. The Oklahoma City bombing was the worst terrorist incident to ever take place in the United States. The 1996 bombing in Atlanta during the Olympic Games left 1 person dead and more than 100 wounded.

Throughout the 1970s and '80s, U.S. cultural, diplomatic, economic, and military interests abroad were major targets of terrorism. In the 1990s a similar threat developed. For instance, of the 296 acts of international terrorism in 1996, approximately one-fourth were directed against U.S. targets. In those incidents 24 were killed and 250 wounded.

The United States has been the most popular single target of international terrorism, by both state-sponsored groups (e.g., Libya, Iraq, and Iran) and substate groups, including Marxist-oriented (Germany's Red Army Faction), Islamic fundamentalist (Hezbollah), Palestinian (Abu Nidal Organization), and ideological mercenary (Japanese Red Army). Other significant attacks against the United States involving foreigners or Americans during the past three decades include: the 1979 takeover of the U.S. Embassy in Tehran, during which American diplomats were held hostage for 444 days; the bombing of the U.S. Embassy and Marine headquarters in Beirut in 1983; the 17-day hijacking of TWA Flight 847 in 1985; the 1988 destruction of Pan Am Flight 103 over Scotland; and the truck bombing at the Khobar Towers near Dhahran, Saudi Arabia, in 1996.

There have also been threats to U.S. embassies in Egypt, Malaysia, and Yemen, to mention a few. Some of them, such as the one in Uganda, have temporarily suspended operations until new security measures are put into place.

In sum, both domestic and international terrorism have touched the lives and interests of individuals and nations in every region of the world. Terrorism has had a substantial impact on the way Americans live, work, and travel abroad. There is also an effect on the way Americans live at home.

Many factors have contributed to the terrorist threat facing the United States. The key factor is that while the United States maintains an extensive cultural, political, economic, and military presence abroad, a number of foreign groups and governments oppose American values, policies, and actions.

In the aftermath of the takeover of the U.S. Embassy in Tehran in 1979 and the bombing of the U.S. Marine barracks in Beirut in 1983, American policymakers have considered terrorism a major threat to national security. In response, Congress passed a "long-arm" statute that makes it a federal crime for a terrorist to threaten, detain, seize, injure, or kill an American citizen abroad. Based on this, the FBI, in a sting operation in international waters off the coast of Cyprus, could arrest Fawaz Younis. Younis, a Lebanese operative implicated in the 1985 hijacking of a Jordanian airliner, which included American hostages, was subsequently convicted and sentenced.

After the Oklahoma City bombing, President Clinton signed the 1996 antiterrorism bill.[5] This legislation provides law enforcement with important new tools to intensify its fight against terrorism. More specifically, this legislation:

- authorizes $1 billion in funding for federal antiterrorism law-enforcement efforts;
- makes it easier for police to trace bombs to the criminals who made them, by requiring chemical taggants in some explosive materials;
- makes it harder for terrorists to raise the money they need to fund their crimes;

---

[7] 1996 antiterrorism bill—Antiterrorism and Effective Death Penalty Act; a sweeping federal law in response to terrorism of the mid-1990s.

- streamlines exclusion and expulsion procedures for terrorist aliens;
- allows the president to withhold foreign aid to countries that provide assistance to any country designated as a supporter of terrorism;
- increases the penalties for conspiracy to commit explosives violations and for specified terrorism-related crimes;
- allows victims of terrorist acts to sue foreign state sponsors of terrorism; and
- expands the use of Victims of Crime Act (VOCA)[8] funds to include terrorism victims.

In 1998, President Clinton used his May 22, 1998, commencement address at the U.S. Naval Academy to unveil a number of new initiatives designed to strengthen American responses to terrorism, such as improving the protection of civilians against the threat of germ warfare. The coming years are likely to see more nations with biological weapons and greater availability of the materials necessary to manufacture such weapons.

The quest by Iraq, Iran, Libya, and North Korea to gain these weapons only confirms such dangers, and **proliferation**[9] increases the opportunities for superterrorism. Prevention and response to biological terrorism is therefore drawing an increasing level of policy attention to and funding for U.S. technologies.

Aborting a biological terrorist attack—whether by preventing the production of the agent, uncovering preparation for an attack, or searching for a device prior to its use—is difficult. In contrast, much can be done to provide those who must respond to such an event with the tools they need to manage its consequences.

---

[8] Victims of Crime Act (VOCA)—program that gives funding, support, and technical assistance to public or private agencies that offer a range of services to victims of crime, including crisis intervention, counseling, guidance, legal advocacy, and transportation to court or to shelters.

[9] **proliferation**—spread.

Government teams that must deter such threats will need greater capabilities to:

- detect and identify the biological agents involved;
- disarm or destroy the device responsible, if it has not yet completed dispersing the agent;
- protect victims and themselves from further contamination;
- track the agent cloud or otherwise delimit the contaminated area;
- decontaminate and treat victims; and
- decontaminate the affected site.

The U.S. government is developing a number of technologies and systems to meet these needs. In addition, under the Nunn-Lugar-Domenici Amendment to the Fiscal Year 1997 Defense Authorization Act, it is developing a program to train those who must respond to biological terrorist attacks. Also, the legislation lends them the expertise and assistance of the Department of Defense. Although we can never eliminate the possibility of a biological terrorist attack, these activities are substantially improving the U.S. government's ability to respond to such threats.

Many governments and people have failed to appreciate the magnitude and implications of the terrorist threat. Some tend to regard it as a minor nuisance. Others simply lack the resources or face what they consider more pressing problems. As a result, a large number of countries have not yet developed a plan to deal effectively with terrorism.

On the other hand, some countries, such as the United States, have taken a variety of effective counter-terrorism measures. These include: improved intelligence-gathering resources against terrorists; appropriate legislation; apprehension, prosecution, and punishment of terrorists; and greater protection for governmental facilities and officials.

The policy implications are threefold:

First, there are no simplistic or complete solutions to the dangers of terrorism. Since the tactics used to challenge the authority of the state are new, so too must be the response by the state. We must also be cautious to avoid the kinds of overreaction that could lead to repression and the ultimate weakening of the democratic institutions that we seek to protect.

Second, having achieved considerable tactical success during the past three decades, terrorists sometimes find it politically expedient to restrain the level of political violence. These self-imposed restraints will not persist indefinitely, and future incidents may continue to be costly in terms of human lives and property. Certain conditions, such as religious extremism or perceptions that the "cause" is lost, could provide terrorists with an incentive to escalate their attacks dramatically.

Third, the vulnerability of modern society and its infrastructure, coupled with the opportunities for using sophisticated, high-leverage conventional and unconventional weaponry, require a credible response to terrorism and the ability to minimize future threats.

QUESTIONS TO CONSIDER

1. What three reasons does the author give to support his view that terrorism will grow in the future?

2. How does the author characterize "superterrorism"?

3. What are some examples that show that terrorists may use chemical, biological, and other nonconventional weapons?

4. Why has America been a prime target for international terrorists since the 1970s?

5. Why does the author feel that "there are no simplistic or complete solutions to the dangers of terrorism"?

Israel and Palestine—Two Kinds of Terrorism

The major terrorist conflict of the last 30 years has been between the Palestinians, who are seeking their own national state, and Israel, which was founded in Palestine in 1948. In a series of wars, the Arab states and the Palestinians did all they could to eradicate the Jewish state. After it won the Six Day War in 1967, Israel occupied the territories where the Palestinians had been living— the West Bank of the Jordan River and the narrow Gaza Strip. Defeated and stateless, the Palestinians turned to terrorism to fight the Israelis. Airline hijackings and bombings, kidnapping and assassination were the means. Israel fought back with all the weapons at its disposal: sealing off the Palestinians in the occupied territories, assassinating militant leaders, and restricting the Palestinians' ability to work and trade. Each labels the other a terrorist as it seeks to influence the Western media. An article that appeared on August 8, 2001, in The Washington Times, *analyzes the attempt of both sides to use the word* terrorist.

On June 1, a Palestinian man wandered into a crowd of young Israelis waiting to enter a Tel Aviv[1] dance club. Just before midnight, the bomb strapped to his midriff exploded, riddling the club-goers with ball bearings and bolts.

Nineteen Israelis and the bomber died that night. Three more Israelis later died of their injuries.

During nearly a year of Israeli-Palestinian strife, the dance-club bombing stands out as the deadliest instance of a certain kind of political violence.

"It was terrorism, because what *terrorism* means is an attack on innocent civilians," said Lianne Elias, a Canadian-Israeli college student who was several blocks away when the bomb exploded. The next day, a mixture of curiosity and **condolence**[2] drew her to the scene.

"But on the other hand, I see that as a half-truth," she continued, standing near the discarded wrapper of a surgical glove. "Because it's the only way the Palestinians have to fight against Israel."

After 11 months of strife, the Israeli-Palestinian conflict is increasingly defined by "terrorism"—both the act and the **epithet**.[3]

The Palestinian uprising, or intifada,[4] began last year with mass demonstrations of Palestinian frustration with the unfulfilled promises of the peace process. But in recent months, the intifada has devolved into attacks on Israeli soldiers and civilians that mix elements of terrorism and guerrilla warfare.

On the Israeli side, the country's leaders endlessly cite "Palestinian terrorism" to justify a stranglehold on

---

[1] Tel Aviv—city on the Mediterranean Sea that is Israel's largest urban center.

[2] **condolence**—feeling of sympathy.

[3] **epithet**—name.

[4] intifada—Palestinian uprising against Israeli occupation that began in September 2000. This recent violence is sometimes referred to as the "Al Aqsa Intifada" to distinguish it from the earlier Palestinian uprising of 1987–1993.

the Palestinian territories, summary executions of reputed militants, and other measures that Palestinians say add up to "state terror."

On both sides of the conflict, there are echoes of the past in this near-obsession with terrorism.

Despite the Palestine Liberation Organization's[5] 1988 renunciation of armed struggle, some Palestinian groups insist on perpetrating acts of violence that are broadly considered terrorist. With each blast or shooting, a little bit of Palestinian legitimacy seems to seep away.

Attacks on its civilians have long allowed Israel to cast the conflict as a battle for security in the face of the scourge of terrorism, rather than as a struggle between peoples with competing claims to the same land.

As Israeli Defense Minister Binyamin Ben Eliezer recently told reporters, "I am not fighting against the Palestinians; I am fighting against terror."

Perhaps no word in modern political usage is more controversial than "terrorism." The United Nations spent 17 years trying to come up with a universally accepted definition, and failed.

In the West and particularly in the United States, it is used to describe political groups that stoop to barbarism to advance their agenda. But the Arabs and Muslims who have often been on the receiving end of the word contend that the "terrorist" label unjustly **vilifies**[6] them and their causes.

They insist that "one man's terrorist is another man's freedom fighter" and that an 18th-century American revolutionary would surely have been a terrorist in British eyes. They argue that the label is used to smear legitimate movements of resistance and national liberation whose interests do not mesh with the West's.

---

[5] Palestine Liberation Organization—or PLO, nationalist group dedicated to the establishment of an independent state for Palestinians in the Middle East.

[6] **vilifies**—makes to seem wrong or evil.

The Web site of an Israeli terrorism think-tank offers this definition: "The intentional use of, or threat to use, violence against civilians or against civilian targets, in order to attain political aims." This wording contains the three elements found in many attempts to define the concept: violence, civilians, and politics.

At a July 1 Tel Aviv University seminar on terrorism and war crimes, some participants argued that a terrorist act can be recognized on its face.

"In deciding whether something is terrorism, you do not ask about the rights or justice of the cause on either side—you only look at what was done," said Max Singer, an Israeli-American public-policy researcher who divides time between the United States and Israel. Other intellectuals have long argued that acts of political violence have to be considered in light of what brings people to engage in them.

Edward Said, a Columbia University professor of literature who is a defender of the Palestinian cause, wrote in 1996 that "terrorism is bred out of poverty, desperation, a sense of powerlessness and utter misery: it signals the failure of politics and vision."

In much the same way, Palestinian spokesmen emphasize context in discussing their militancy. "We don't justify killing people, but we do justify defending ourselves," says Ismail Abu Shanab, a U.S.-educated engineering instructor in the Gaza Strip and a spokesman for Hamas,[7] a Palestinian party whose militants have killed scores of Israeli civilians.

Mr. Abu Shanab says that Hamas' operations are a reaction to Israel's military-enforced occupation of Palestinian lands, its retaliatory strikes against targets held by the Palestinians, its strategy of assassinating

---

[7] Hamas—Arabic word for "zeal," this organization was formed in 1987 by those who maintain that, as an Islamic homeland, no part of Palestine can ever be occupied by non-Muslims. Opposing the 1993 peace agreement between the PLO and Israel, Hamas's armed wing launched a terrorist campaign against Israel that included the use of suicide bombers.

Palestinian militants, and the "closures" of towns and villages that choke off Palestinian economic life.

"If you hit Palestinian civilians," he said, "you can't expect your own civilians to be safe." His organization claimed responsibility for the bombing at the Tel Aviv dance club.

Many Palestinians say the Israeli measures amount to state terrorism. Palestinians fear being killed in an Israeli military strike, just as Israelis worry about dying at the hands of a Palestinian suicide bomber. Since the uprising began in September, more than 500 people have been killed on the Palestinian side and more than 100 on the Israeli side.

Israeli officials concede that their actions and policies have resulted in the deaths of innocent Palestinian civilians, but argue that Israel is only defending itself against a Palestinian negotiating strategy that now prominently features violence. Palestinian attacks, particularly those inside Israel proper, are something different, the Israelis say: indiscriminate strikes against civilians that are designed to instill fear.

The Israelis haven't always been on the receiving end alone. Writers such as Mr. Said and Patrick Seale, a British journalist with long experience in the Mideast, argue that Jewish groups active before the founding of the Israeli state brought the practice to the region.

In the 1930s and 1940s, as Zionists[8] were buying land in what was then known as Palestine, Arabs often rioted against their settlements and attacked Jews on the roads. Vigilante groups arose to retaliate on behalf of the Zionists, often with devastating results.

After a spate of individual killings of Jews in 1938, writes the British historian Martin Gilbert, "on July 6, a

---

[8] Zionists—followers of Zionism, a political movement begun formally by Austrian Theodor Herzl, who in 1897 helped draft a mission statement that read, "Zionism strives to create for the Jewish people a home in Palestine secured by public law." This goal was reached in 1948.

single Jewish terrorist bomb killed 25 Arabs in Haifa." The killings continued, and less than three weeks later, a Jewish bomb killed 39 Arabs in Haifa's melon market.

More recently, in 1994, an Israeli settler killed 29 Palestinians praying in a mosque in Hebron, and earlier this month, an Israeli group called the "Committee for Road Safety" claimed responsibility for the apparently random killing of two Palestinian men and their 15-week-old relative.

Despite these events, Israel has successfully portrayed itself as a victim, not a perpetrator, of terrorism. By the mid-1980s, writes Mr. Seale, "Israel had won wide acceptance for its version of the Arab-Israeli dispute: the violence of its opponents was 'terror.' Its own was 'legitimate self-defense.'"

This trend is even more pronounced today. "It's fair to say that Israel describes any attack against it as terrorism," said Mark Heller, deputy director of the Jaffee Center for Strategic Studies at Tel Aviv University.

In February, a Palestinian bus driver drove his Israeli bus into a bus stop full of waiting soldiers, killing seven of them and one civilian. The Israeli media labeled the event a "terror attack" despite the driver's apparent intent to kill soldiers. "When they kill Israeli soldiers," said Mr. Singer, referring to Palestinian attackers, "it isn't terrorism, it's guerrilla warfare."

The Israelis portray the Palestinians as terrorists in part because it helps the country overcome what the Israelis have long seen as an image problem—the fact that they dramatically overpower the Palestinians in terms of military strength and economic power.

At a second Tel Aviv University seminar in July, this one on the strategic use of the media, a top Israeli general named Giora Eiland noted that "we are not the weaker party, nor do we want to be."

David-and-Goliath analogies ought to be discarded in favor of a sheriff-vs.-outlaws scenario, Maj. Gen. Eiland suggested. "The sheriff is allowed to be stronger because the other side is criminal," he said. "There is no limit to how much you can explain how evil the other side is."

Emphasizing "Palestinian terrorism" also helps Israel find friends abroad in a world that has been broadly supportive of U.N. resolutions concerning the Palestinian claim to the West Bank and Gaza Strip. Most governments are concerned about terrorism of one kind or another, so rising in support of a people who are constantly described as "terrorists" is no easy matter.

The antidote to terrorism, in the Israeli view, is security. "Terrorism is a form of warfare, and if it's going to be addressed at all, it needs to be addressed as a security threat," said Mr. Heller of the Jaffee Center.

Even though a mid-June poll found that nearly 69 percent of Palestinians say that suicide attacks are a "suitable response" to "current political conditions," some question the wisdom of engaging in such acts.

In early June, a Palestinian journalist and Ministry of Information official named Muhammad Abdelhamid argued in the daily newspaper *al-Ayyam* that suicide operations were illegal and counterproductive.

"The question that poses itself in this regard is whether Israeli repression, the practice of targeting Palestinian civilians, and the imposition of collective punishments allow us to abandon our commitment to universal humanitarian standards in our dealings with Israeli civilians? The answer is 'No,'" Mr. Abdelhamid wrote. "Commitment is an indication of strength, an expression of a moral and humanistic superiority, and in addition, it serves to win world public opinion to our side."

Abed Rahim Mallouh, a member of the executive committee of the Palestine Liberation Organization, offers a gentle critique of the suicide operations carried out by Hamas and another group, Islamic Jihad.[9] "The PFLP," he said, referring to his own party, the Popular Front for the Liberation of Palestine,[10] "is not in favor of such actions, but I understand why people are doing such things."

After years of dormancy,[11] the PFLP reactivated its military wing a half-year ago. Its members eschew[12] suicide tactics and attacks against civilians. They prefer targets identified with the state of Israel or its security forces.

---

[9] Islamic Jihad—fundamentalist group that has used terrorism in Israel and the Palestinian occupied territories to disrupt or halt the peace process between Israel and the Palestinians.

[10] Popular Front for the Liberation of Palestine—organization that since 1967 has dedicated itself to the elimination of the state of Israel and is not open to compromise. The PFLP has undertaken many acts of terrorism, including hijacking Israeli planes starting in the late 1960s.

[11] dormancy—inactivity.

[12] eschew—avoid.

QUESTIONS TO CONSIDER

1. What are some examples of violence against civilians being carried out by both Jews and Muslims in the Middle East?

2. Why do Israel and the Palestinians seek to identify each other as "terrorists"?

3. How might Palestinians see Israeli forces, rather than their own suicide bombers, as the true terrorists?

4. What might be counterproductive about a government labeling "any attack" against its country as "terrorist"?

The New Terrorist

BY EHUD SPRINZAK

Most terrorists have little to gain from mass destruction. It would only bring them the world's repulsion instead of support for their cause. But over the last decade, a new breed of terrorist has arisen, mostly based on religious belief in a coming catastrophe. The goals of the "new terrorism" differ from the politically motivated terrorism of nationalists and anti-capitalists. Because their goals are unachievable, these terrorists do not worry about the reaction of the world at large to their attacks. As a former head of the CIA said, they "don't want a seat at the table, they want to destroy the table and everyone sitting at it." Attacks like Timothy McVeigh's in Oklahoma City, the gas attack in Tokyo by the Aum Shinrikyo, or the ones organized by Osama bin Laden are the work of people with a vision of an enemy, but no interest in the future. In a 2001 article in Foreign Policy, *political scientist Ehud Sprinzak examines the rise of what he calls the "hyperterrorist."*

Shortly following the September 11 terrorist attacks on American soil, U.S. Sen. Richard Shelby, vice chairman of the Senate Intelligence Committee, offered a now widespread view when he blamed the tragedy on a "massive intelligence failure" by the United States. Indeed, many critics point to a series of institutional or operational failings: inadequate funding for intelligence activities, a **dearth**[1] of Arabic-speaking agents, and insufficient international intelligence-sharing and cross-border cooperation. Yet the inability to foresee the latest attacks exposes a problem well beyond poor intelligence gathering. Rather, it reveals an intellectual failure to identify an entirely new category of terrorism. Our post-September 11 comprehension of terrorism must recognize a new enemy: the megalomaniacal[2] hyperterrorist.

Many of the devastating acts of terror that took place in the 1990s were masterminded by innovative, self-anointed individuals with larger-than-life callings. Ramzi Yousef (the man behind the 1993 World Trade Center bombing), Shoko Asahara (leader of Aum Shinrikyo and architect of the 1995 gas attack in a Tokyo subway station), Timothy McVeigh (the 1995 Oklahoma City bomber), and Osama bin Laden (likely planner of the September 11 **carnage**[3]) are linked by their insatiable urge to use catastrophic attacks in order to write a new chapter in history. Call it the "Great Man" theory of terrorism. Yigal Amir, the 1995 assassin of Israeli Prime Minister Yitzhak Rabin,[4] also belongs on this list. Amir may not have been involved in mass-casualty terrorism, but the impact of his act on the Israeli people could not have been more catastrophic.

Certainly, the history of terrorism is littered with forceful personalities and charismatic leaders, but specialists never thought the study of individual activists could help them understand what they always considered to be a group-oriented phenomenon. Consequently,

---

[1] **dearth**—lack.

[2] megalomaniacal—having delusions of being very powerful.

[3] **carnage**—bloodshed.

[4] Yitzhak Rabin—(1922–1995) prime minister of Israel (1974–1977 and 1992–1995). He was assassinated by a Jewish extremist while attending a peace rally in 1995.

experts classified terrorism along organizational or ideological lines, with revolutionary left-wing, conservative right-wing, separatist-nationalist, and religious terrorism as the typical categories. The 1990s rendered this typology[5] obsolete. In fact, our conceptual disregard for the megalomaniacal hyperterrorist is one of the fundamental reasons for the repeated failures to avert the catastrophes of the last 10 years.

Of course, not all modern-day terrorists fall into this new category. The vast majority of terrorists and terror organizations still behave according to the logic portrayed in hundreds of academic studies, scholarly models, and intelligence profiles. They are political, conservative in their use of weapons, and low-casualty perpetrators. Though angry, lethal, ready to take great personal risks, they are largely rational and realistic. They act in groups or organizations, use the media to get attention, and wish to transform their fights into legitimate military campaigns and political power. They kill, maim, abduct, bomb, and even blow themselves up in suicide missions, but their leaders, ideologues, gurus,[6] and clerics prefer to avoid catastrophes in order to secure sympathy in the post-terrorism stage. As terrorism expert Brian Jenkins famously remarked, such leaders wish to have "lots of people watching, not lots of people dead."

Megalomaniacal hyperterrorists operate according to an altogether different logic. While often working with the support of large terror groups and organizations, they tend to be loners. They think big, seeking to go beyond "conventional" terrorism and, unlike most terrorists, could be willing to use weapons of mass destruction. They perceive themselves in historical terms and dream of individually devastating the hated

---

[5] typology—system of classification.

[6] gurus—personal spiritual teachers or guides in any field, but originally applied to spiritual and philosophical matters.

system. Ramzi Yousef is a classic example: Talking to the FBI agent who arrested him in 1995, Yousef openly discussed his dream of seeing one of the World Trade Center towers fall into the other, causing 250,000 casualties. While hiding in the Philippines in 1995, he planned to destroy 12 U.S. aircraft in midair. Yousef also entertained ideas about using chemical weapons on a large scale.

Or consider Timothy McVeigh, a Gulf War[7] hero turned murderer of 168 innocent men, women, and children. McVeigh viewed himself as the lone defender of America against a violent and illegitimate federal government; he refused to ask for **clemency**[8] and went to his death with a great sense of historical accomplishment. (In his correspondence with writer Gore Vidal, McVeigh compared the justice of his act to the justice behind President Harry Truman's 1945 attack on Hiroshima.[9]) And Yigal Amir, a right-wing resolute loner, believed that he had to "save the people (of Israel) because the people failed to understand the real conditions." Disregarding an entire antigovernment movement, including illustrious settler activists, Amir convinced himself that God wanted him to personally save the nation, and he was ready to die upon the completion of the mission.

Unlike most terrorists, who are technologically conservative, megalomaniacal hyperterrorists are innovators, developers. They incessantly look for original ways to surprise and devastate the enemy. Though not politically blind, they remain apolitical. They know

---

[7] Gulf War—also called the Persian Gulf War (1990–1991), a conflict that began when Iraq under Saddam Hussein invaded and occupied Kuwait. In early 1991, a U.S.-led alliance that included France, Great Britain, Egypt, Saudi Arabia, and Syria attacked Iraqi forces and retook Kuwait.

[8] **clemency**—mercy.

[9] Hiroshima—city in Japan that the United States attacked with an atomic bomb on August 6, 1945, to end World War II.

that their actions will foster public outrage, yet they do not care. They believe history alone will judge them, and they are certain of absolution. They know that their terrorism is likely to bring about their death. Death, life in prison, and massive public condemnation are, in fact, risks worth taking, almost part of their self-selected job description.

The rise of the megalomaniacal hyperterrorist does not mean we should toss out the old antiterrorism manuals. Rather than reinvent counterterrorism measures, we should redirect existing efforts toward this new enemy. The best way to deal with megalomaniacal hyperterrorists is through preemptive military strikes on known terrorists and yes, through increased investments in human intelligence aimed at identifying hitherto unknown or potential megalomaniacal foes. Both approaches require great **elucidation**[10] and development, but both are utterly necessary—now more than ever before.

---

[10] **elucidation**—clarification.

QUESTIONS TO CONSIDER

1. Who are some of the "lone gunmen" the author refers to?

2. What does the author think the "new category of terrorism" is? Why might people have failed to notice it?

3. What is the change in terrorist "logic" that the author points out?

4. Why is the "megalomaniacal hyperterrorist" likely to risk death or life imprisonment?

5. In your opinion, is terrorism typically caused by isolated individuals or by groups? What evidence is there for either side of this argument?

Profile of a Terrorist

BY JIM YARDLEY

It is very hard to define what sort of person chooses to sacrifice his or her life for a cause. Until the attack on the World Trade Center, the majority of suicide bombers had been very young men with fanatical religious views. The wave of suicide bombers in Israel fit this pattern: young men trained for—some would say indoctrinated into—the act of sacrifice. They were promised that they would go straight to paradise and that their families would be taken care of. The attacks of September 11 were by a different breed, more determined and less overtly fanatical. This article from The New York Times *is a portrait of Egyptian Mohamed Atta, one of the main organizers of the attacks.*

Precisely two years ago, not long before he traveled to the United States to coordinate the worst terrorist attacks in history, Mohamed Atta attended a wedding. The event was held in the German port city of Hamburg, where Mr. Atta had recently earned a university degree, but this was not the marriage of a college friend.

The groom was Said Bahaji, now the focus of an international manhunt for his suspected role in the Sept. 11

attacks. Prominent among the guests was Mamoun Darkazanli, a Syrian businessman suspected of being a financial **conduit**[1] for Osama bin Laden's al-Qaeda organization. Another guest was Mr. Atta's friend, Marwan al-Shehhi, whom authorities say crashed the second hijacked airliner into the World Trade Center.

This was not what Mr. Atta's father in Egypt had imagined when he sent his son abroad to earn the sort of academic degree that would bring him prestige and success at home. Instead of becoming an architect or an urban planner, Mr. Atta had become an Islamic terrorist.

Mr. Atta's path to Sept. 11, pieced together from interviews with people who knew him across 33 years and three continents, was a quiet and methodical evolution of resentment that somehow—and that how remains the essential imponderable—took a leap to mass-murderous fury.

The youngest child of a pampering mother and an ambitious father, Mr. Atta was a polite, shy boy who came of age in an Egypt torn between growing Western influence and the religious fundamentalism that gathered force in reaction. But it was not until he was on his own, in the West, that his religious faith deepened and his resentments hardened. The focus of his disappointment became the Egyptian government; the target of his blame became the West, and especially America.

In Hamburg, his life divided into before and after. He would disappear more than once, and officials say they have strong evidence that he trained at Mr. bin Laden's terrorist camps in Afghanistan during the late 1990s. It was also in those years, German investigators say, that Mr. Atta became part of the Hamburg cell[2] that became a key planning point for the Sept. 11 attacks.

"I remember that he changed somewhat," said Dittmar Machule, his academic supervisor at Hamburg

---

[1] **conduit**—channel.

[2] cell—smallest organizational unit of a centralized group or movement.

Technical University. "He looked more serious, and he didn't smile as much."

His acquaintances from that time still cannot reconcile him as a killer, but in hindsight the raw ingredients of his personality suggest some clues. He was **meticulous**,[3] disciplined and highly intelligent.

His vision of Islam embraced resolute **precepts**[4] of fate and destiny and purity, and, ultimately, tolerated no compromise. He ate no pork and scraped the frosting off cakes, in case it contained lard. He threatened to leave the university unless he was given a room for a prayer group. He spoke of a desire to marry, but was remote to the point of rudeness with women, considering most insufficiently devout.

Those who had known him as a quiet student say his **demeanor**[5] became more brooding, more troubled. The most obvious change was both cosmetic and spiritual: he had grown the beard of an Islamic fundamentalist.

The genteel gloss of the Abdein neighborhood of Cairo[6] had dulled to shabby disrepair by the early 1980s when Mohamed al-Amir Atta entered his teenage years. The government workers who had once lived well on $100 a month found themselves in a vortex of downward mobility, working second and third jobs to survive.

Mr. Atta's father, a lawyer, considered his neighbors inferior, even if he, too, feared the economic undertow. Neighbors recalled an arrogant man who often passed without a word or a glance.

The family was viewed as thoroughly modern, the two daughters headed for careers as a professor and a doctor. The father was the disciplinarian, grumbling that

---

[3] **meticulous**—extremely careful with details.

[4] **precepts**—rules or principles prescribing a particular course of action or conduct.

[5] **demeanor**—manner.

[6] Cairo—capital of Egypt.

his wife spoiled their bright, if timid, son, who continued to sit on her lap until enrolling at Cairo University.

"I used to tell her that she is raising him as a girl, and that I have three girls, but she never stopped pampering him," Mohamed al-Amir Atta, Sr., recalled in a recent interview at his apartment.

In a high school classroom of 26 students grouped by their shared given name, Mohammed Hassan Attiya recalled that Mr. Atta focused solely on becoming an engineer—and following his father's bidding.

"I never saw him playing," Mr. Attiya said. "We did not like him very much, and I think he wanted to play with the rest of the boys, but his family, and I think his father, wanted him to always perform in school in an excellent way."

The social, political and religious pressures roiling Egypt exploded in 1981 with the assassination of President Anwar el-Sadat,[7] the first Arab leader to make peace with Israel. Fundamentalists decried him as a puppet of the West, a traitor to Islam.

Even for a boy as sheltered as Mr. Atta, the disillusionment on the streets would have been difficult to ignore. His father, without explanation, says his son began to pray in earnest at 12 or 13, an awakening that coincided closely with Sadat's slaying. But the elder Mr. Atta said his son's religious inclination did not extend to politics.

"I advised him, like my father advised me, that politics equals hypocrisy," his father said.

The boy refused to join a basketball league because it was organized by the Muslim Brotherhood, Egypt's most established religious political organization, which also recruited from Cairo University's engineering

---

[7] Anwar el-Sadat—(1918–1981) president of Egypt (1970–1981). In 1973, he led his country to join Syria in an attack on Israel. Four years later, however, he became part of a historic diplomatic process with Israel that resulted in his being a co-recipient of the Nobel Peace Prize in 1978 and signing the first peace treaty between Israel and an Arab nation in 1979. He was assassinated by Muslim extremists.

department but not, apparently, Mr. Atta, who graduated from there in 1990.

His degree meant little in a country where thousands of college graduates were unable to find good jobs. Though Mr. Atta found work with a German company in Cairo and was reluctant to leave his mother and sisters, his father convinced him that only an advanced degree from abroad would allow him to prosper in Egypt. Soon he was headed to Hamburg Technical University on scholarship.

"I told him I needed to hear the word 'doctor' in front of his name," his father recalled. "We told him your sisters are doctors and their husbands are doctors and you are the man of the family."

From initial appearances, the slender young Mr. Atta remained the same person in Hamburg that he had been in Egypt—polite, distant and neatly dressed. He answered a classified ad and was hired part-time at an urban planning firm, Plankontor. He impressed his co-workers with his diligence and the careful elegance of his drafting.

Yet he must have felt unmoored, on his own in a strange land. He took refuge in the substantial population of Turkish, African, and Arab immigrants living in the blue-collar Harburg section surrounding the university. There, his religious faith, still tentative in Egypt, took deeper hold.

He brought a prayer carpet to his job and carefully adhered to Islamic dietary restrictions, shunning alcohol and checking the ingredients of everything, even medicine. He had his choice of three mosques, but the two closest to campus were dominated by Turks, whom many local Arabs disdained as less devout and too sympathetic to America.

Instead, Mr. Atta often prayed at the Arabic-language Al-Tauhid mosque, a bleak back room of a small shop where the imam,[8] Ahmed Emam, preached that America was an enemy of Islam and a country "unloved in our world."

Mr. Atta's academic focus was Arab cities, specifically preserving them in the face of Western-style development. He returned to Cairo for three months in 1995 to observe a renovation project around the old city gates, Bab Al-Nasr and Bab Al-Futuh. The project, he came to believe, involved little more than knocking down a poor neighborhood to improve the views for tourists.

"It made him angry," recalled Ralph Bodenstein, one of two German students in the program. "He said it was a completely absurd way to develop the city, to make a Disneyworld out of it."

Over meals with Mr. Bodenstein and the other German student, Volker Hauth, Mr. Atta spoke bitterly about the government's suppression of Islamic fundamentalist groups and the clinics and day care centers they had built in ignored neighborhoods.

His sympathy for their cause, Mr. Atta feared, would doom his own future at home. His only hope for a good urban-planning job in Egypt was to be hired by an international organization. He tried but never was. The young man sent West to better his future at home now worried that he had no future in Egypt at all.

He returned to Hamburg in 1996, and investigators say he eventually moved into an apartment at 54 Marienstrasse with two other suspected hijackers, Mr. al-Shehhi and Ziad Jarrah.

In November 1997 he paid an unexpected visit to his academic supervisor, Professor Machule, to discuss his **thesis**,[9] then disappeared again for about a year. Federal officials say they have strong evidence that he trained at

---

[8] imam—Arabic word for "leader," term used for the head of a Muslim community.

[9] **thesis**—essay written by a candidate for an academic degree.

an al-Qaeda camp in Afghanistan during the late 1990s, which could explain his whereabouts in 1998.

He reappeared in Hamburg in early 1999, the period that German investigators connect him with the cell of about 20 other suspected terrorists. At the university, he insisted on a room for an Islamic prayer group. A student council representative **demurred**,[10] suspicious that such organizations were cover for terrorist recruitment.

"He said, 'This is about my life. If I cannot pray here, I cannot study here, at this university,'" said the council representative, Marcus Meyer.

Mr. Atta's degree had been on hold: suddenly, finishing it became imperative. He submitted his thesis in August 1999. When he successfully defended his thesis, graduating with high honors, Mr. Atta refused to shake hands with one of the two judges, a woman.

His father has told reporters that his son earned a master's degree in Germany, but in fact, Mr. Atta received only an undergraduate degree. But his attentions were already elsewhere. He began preparing to go to America.

With few exceptions, Mohamed Atta regarded the Americans who crossed his path with the same contempt his father once reserved for his Cairo neighbors. He was polite when he had to be—to rent a car or an airplane—but the mildness recalled by his friends in Egypt and Germany was gone, as was his beard.

He arrived in June at Newark International Airport and would spend the next 15 months in near perpetual motion, earning a pilot's license in Florida during the last six months of 2000, then spending the first nine months of 2001 traveling across the country and at least twice to Europe.

---

[10] **demurred**—objected.

The awful efficiency of the attack demanded a leader with a precise and disciplined temperament, and Mr. Atta apparently filled that role. Federal investigators have told a House committee that in the fall of 2000, as he was in the middle of flight training in Venice, Fla., Mr. Atta received a wire transfer of more than $100,000 from a source in the United Arab Emirates.[11] Investigators believe the source was Mustafa Ahmad, thought to be an alias for Shaykh Said, a finance chief for Mr. bin Laden.

For much of 2001, Mr. Atta appeared to make important contacts with other hijackers or conspirators. He traveled twice to Spain, in January and July, and officials are investigating whether he met with al-Qaeda contacts. He also used Florida as a base to move around the United States, including trips to Atlanta, where he rented a plane, to New Jersey, where he may have met with other hijackers, and at least two trips to Las Vegas. Everywhere he went, he made hundreds of cell phone calls and made a point to rent computers for e-mails, including at a Las Vegas computer store, Cyberzone, where customers can play a video game about terrorists with a voice that declares "terrorists win."

While Mr. Atta was considered a perfectionist, he was not **infallible**.[12] Brad Warrick, owner of a rental agency in South Florida where Mr. Atta returned a car two days before the attack, found an ATM receipt and a white Post-it note that became key evidence. Mr. Atta's decision to wire $4,000 overseas shortly before the attacks left an electronic trail that investigators believe is leading back to al-Qaeda. Finally, authorities found his luggage at Logan Airport in Boston, containing, among other things, his will. It remains unclear if the bag simply missed the connection to his flight.

---

[11] United Arab Emirates—country along the Persian Gulf on the Arabian Peninsula. It contains about one-tenth of the world's oil reserves.

[12] **infallible**—incapable of making a mistake.

Or perhaps the introvert, the meticulous planner, the man who believed he was doing God's will, wanted to make certain the world knew his name.

QUESTIONS TO CONSIDER

1. What are the basic factors the author feels were present in Atta's life that led him to become a terrorist? What is your opinion of the importance of these factors?

2. How did Atta's upbringing and political events in his childhood help shape his personality?

3. How might Atta's studies on the preservation of Arab cities have intensified his political hatred of the West?

4. How might a sense of having "no future" turn someone toward a path of terrorism?

5. Why does the author speculate that Atta may have wanted the world to know his name after his death?

One-year-old Baylee Almon was pronounced dead shortly after being carried by fireman Chris Fields from the Oklahoma City Federal Building bombing. The photograph won the 1995 Pulitzer Prize. ▶

Coping with Terrorism

▲

Castine Deveroux's five children await word on their mother, who worked in the Oklahoma City federal building.

Medical crews rush to the scene of the bomb explosion in Oklahoma City. ▶

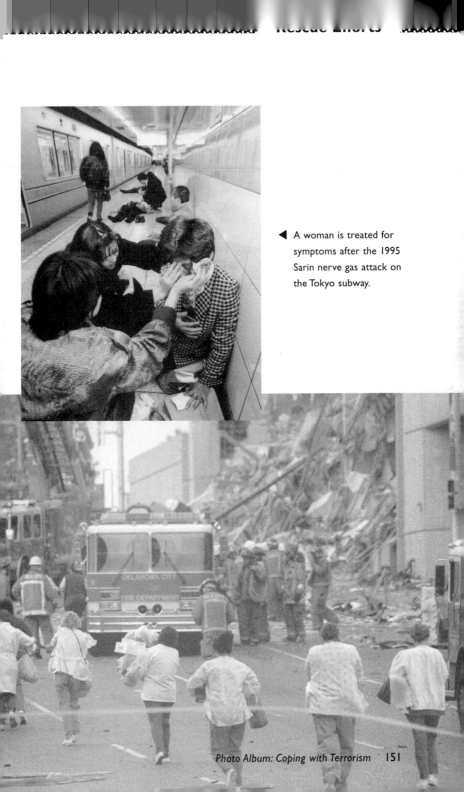

◀ A woman is treated for symptoms after the 1995 Sarin nerve gas attack on the Tokyo subway.

A woman mourns at a poster of assassinated Indian prime minister Rajiv Gandhi.

The mother of one of the slain Israeli athletes at the 1972 Munich Olympics reacts to her loss.

▲
A woman holds a candle during a peace demonstration against Michael
McKevitt, alleged leader of a breakaway IRA group responsible for the 1998
car bombing in the Northern Ireland city of Omagh.

Outside a fund-raiser for IRA prisoners, protesters hold up posters showing those murdered in the 1998 car bombing.

▼

Tens of thousands of youths parade down a street in Rome protesting the kidnapping of former Italian premier Aldo Moro and the slaying of his five bodyguards.

▼

▲
Workers begin to clean up after the Oklahoma City bombing.

The army cleans up a Tokyo subway car after the 1995 nerve gas attack.
▼

part three

Responding as a Nation

What Is the Right Response?

Following September 11, there was no national consensus on what should be done, but there was a decided feeling throughout the United States that the world had changed, that things must be different. The 1941 attack on Pearl Harbor is the only other such moment in modern American history, and the response then was simple: the government declared war, and every man, woman, and child pitched in. This time it was not so simple. Every American may have felt like a target—for this was a random attack on civilians. But there was no obvious enemy to strike out at. What came to the fore in the weeks after the attack was the true American identity: the shared values, freedoms, and hopes for the future that unite all Americans. There was a great stirring of patriotism and gratitude for the ideals that were established in this nation at its founding. These ideals are ones that can never grow old or be defeated. They are, in Thomas Jefferson's words, the unalienable rights to "life, liberty, and the pursuit of happiness." A September 2001 article from U.S. News & World Report surveys some of the reactions to the attacks.

"Everything will be different from now on." Or so says Tom Edelmann, a lawyer for a St. Louis bank. The sentiment was repeated again and again last week. As the horror sank in—and the enormity of the attacks came into focus—Americans from all over the country and all walks of life sensed that their world had changed. Any lingering illusions of national invulnerability were shattered. "I'm realizing life is never going to be the same," says Joseph Wanco, a restaurant owner in Wellfleet, Mass. "It's just a loss of innocence."

A loss of innocence, certainly. But also, possibly, the gain of things more valuable: realism, a sense of national unity and purpose, and even wisdom. Securing those will depend on how Americans respond to the challenges in the weeks, months, and years ahead, and many have already reacted in encouraging ways. From heroic acts of rescue to extensive volunteer efforts to a run on American flags at stores, people are displaying a civic and patriotic spirit that many social analysts had thought was lost.

Cause for hope. Many are turning to faith and sacred traditions for courage and guidance—and finding both. Even custodians of popular culture have shown admirable discretion and restraint, postponing baseball and other national pastimes; Hollywood and the networks have rescheduled violent fare. There have been troubling signs, of course, including senseless and cowardly attacks on Arab-Americans, Muslims, and others. Americans will have to be as wise about the measures they resist as the ones they embrace. But the discernment and good sense that many have shown in the early aftermath of unspeakable horrors give greatest cause for hope beyond the immediate tragedy.

Americans will certainly need all the judgment they can muster as they confront an elusive and problematic foe. "In Pearl Harbor, we knew our enemy, and they struck at the military," says Donald Hunt, 79, a World War II veteran and survivor of that attack. "This time around, we don't know our enemy, and they struck at innocent people." Compounding the problem, says Walter Reich, a professor of international affairs, **ethics**,[1] and human behavior at George Washington University, is that "the enemy here is not a country but a cause without a specific address that is mobilized against us—against our very identity."

That kind of foe creates painful dilemmas. "We're going to have to respond in ways that threaten to undermine the very values and culture that enrage the people who attack us," says Reich. "This forces us to reconsider decisions we have already made—decisions about extrajudicial[2] measures such as assassinations and other actions."

Those decisions are already being reconsidered, both in Congress and in the larger arena of public opinion. Whether intelligence agencies will return to such measures as working with "unsavory" members of terrorist cells remains to be seen. Mel Goodman, a former CIA analyst and now a senior fellow at the Center for International Policy, counsels caution and says that the real intelligence need is more and better analysis of the huge amounts of information. He does admit, however, that he thinks that relying on so many official State Department covers for clandestine information gathering is a waste of human resources. "How are they going to collect information about terrorists when they are working out of embassies?" he asks.

More and more average citizens are resigned to the use of the most aggressive covert measures. "If they could assassinate bin Laden tomorrow, they should use whoever they need to do it," says Tina Rose, 48, a retiree residing in Livermore, Calif. Nathan Pearson, a biology graduate student at the University of Chicago, voices a

---

[1] **ethics**—rules or standards governing the conduct of a person or the members of a profession.

[2] extrajudicial—outside existing laws.

similar view: "I don't see a fundamental difference between that [assassination] and warfare."

But to Andrew Bacevich, professor of international relations at Boston University, it's important to be very clear about what we are responding to. "To talk about this as terrorism pushes the political implications into the background," he says. "It emphasizes the criminality of the act. It's not appropriate to call it an act of terrorism; [it is] an act of war." Since wars are about political objectives, he explains, America's response should not be on pursuing justice but on achieving political objectives. "Which raises a big question," says Bacevich: "What are our political objectives?" If they include supporting a global system compatible with American values, he concludes, "It would be a massive mistake to think that simply bombing someone would be a successful response."

Duty calls. A more sustained response of the kind that Bacevich and, indeed, President Bush call for will require a stronger sense of patriotic duty and obligation than most Americans have shown in recent years. While it is too early to say that it will last, such patriotism has taken a sudden and sharp turn upward. "In the wake of this week's events, I have had three different students in my office asking about where they would go and what they would study to become an FBI or NSA[3] agent," says Beth Karling, a guidance counselor at Mater Dei High School in Santa Ana, Calif. Military recruiters also report a surge in calls from people wanting to enlist, even from some who are long past enlistment age. Andy Bernard, 25, an aspiring writer and actor in Los Angeles, has been surprised by the awakening of his sense of duty. "I would gladly defend my country, which is interesting because in the past I have said that I don't believe

---

[3] NSA—National Security Agency, federal government agency with responsibility for protecting U.S. military information systems and gathering foreign intelligence information.

in war. Now I don't think I would lose sleep over having to kill someone who was responsible for this." At the very least, many young Americans now look critically on their own former political **apathy**.[4] "We have an obligation to take a more active role," says Lisa Jacobs, a first-year student at Harvard Business School.

Even as they think about what they must do differently, Americans are concerned not to change some things too much. In the short term, this means not rescheduling weddings long planned for the weekend following the attack, for example; many consider postponing major life events to be the same thing as letting the terrorists win. In the longer run, returning to life as usual means recognizing and respecting the strong **libertarian**[5] tradition valued by many Americans. James McQuivey, research director at Forrester Research in Cambridge, Mass., says, "We're just too fiercely independent [to give up civil liberties]. I'm not sure they're going to persuade the public that's necessary." He points out that the government already has extensive powers of **surveillance**[6] that infringe upon privacy. "It's not like they wanted to tap somebody's phone and couldn't," he says.

"There's a fine line between safety and individual rights," says Todd Longsworth, an attorney in Boston, "and I hope maintaining that line won't be too hard." It need not be, says University of Chicago legal scholar Richard Epstein, if people think more clearly about what the state should do in the execution of its most important responsibility: protecting citizens from those who use force or fraud against them. "People are already starting to talk about increasing security measures and putting more controls over citizens. Why not arm pilots

---

[4] **apathy**—lack of interest or concern.

[5] **libertarian**—concerned with the protection of those rights guaranteed to the individual by law.

[6] **surveillance**—close observation of a person or group, especially one under suspicion.

or air marshals?" he asks. "If we had a more coherent program, we'd have more people trained to use arms to protect us from rogues and terrorists. We can lose a lot of freedoms and gain nothing, or we can meet the threat of force with force."

Fears. Some Americans also recognize the need to guard against depriving the rights of some citizens in the name of national security. "We should think about how poorly we handled our fears in the past," says historian Alan Brinkley, citing the internment of Japanese-Americans during World War II as one of America's least glorious hours. "We all feel under attack—all of us Americans are under attack, and it's time to huddle together," says Maher Hathout, a cardiologist and spokesman for Muslim rights in Arcadia, Calif. "I'm always afraid of the ignorant. Always, in every society, there are fanatics and ignorant people who can react in unpredictable ways. When there's hype and **innuendoes**[7] and premature actions, anything can happen."

But maybe there are signs of hope even where fear tends to rule. "The press has been more objective," says Farkhunda Ali, communications director of the American Muslim Council in Washington, D.C. "Ever since we found out that the real perpetrators of the Oklahoma City bombing weren't Muslim, the press is being more objective—at this time anyway."

Handling fears may be the most profound challenge of all, and America's religious leaders have taken a conspicuous lead. "My experience has been that people who never think of God any other time will turn their eyes, or at least their attention, to something outside themselves at a time like this," says the Rev. Peg Cantwell of Westlake Hills Presbyterian Church in Austin, which offered two special prayer services on the day of the attacks. She received a phone call from a man who

---

[7] **innuendoes**—hints or suggestions.

couldn't reach relatives in New York City, asking her to pray for them during the services. "He said, 'Can you just mention their names? Can you just say their names?'"

Before long, Cantwell expects to be fielding questions from parishioners whose faith in God was shaken by the tragedy of last week's attacks. "It's normal to be angry at God," she says. "If somebody comes to me in that mode, all I'd want to say is tell the Lord, 'If you're there, I'm angry at you.' But the thing I'd like to try to help them not do is shut God out."

Coming up with answers is not easy, even for a religious thinker well known for helping ordinary people make sense of tragedy. "I'm as stunned and amazed as anyone," says Rabbi Harold Kushner, author of *When Bad Things Happen to Good People*. Still, Kushner has an answer to the age-old question: How can a just God permit evil to flourish? "We believe in Judaism that God has given human beings the choice to opt for doing good or doing evil." But Kushner does not believe that this is the moment to get into elaborate theological explanations of why God gave people free will. The proper religious response now, he says, "is to dry the tears and hold the hands of people who have suffered losses." Michael Manning, a Catholic priest and host of the television show *The Word in the World*, speaks more assertively of the need to fight evil, even while acknowledging the painful truth that Christians in the past, during the Inquisition[8] and the Crusades,[9] allowed themselves to lose touch with the "God of love and patience and love for all."

Americans learned to balance their ideals of forgiveness and justice many times in their past. Their foes might consider how quickly they are forcing Americans to do so again.

---

[8] Inquisition—Roman Catholic courts for investigating and prosecuting charges of heresy, especially the one active in Spain beginning in the 1400s.

[9] Crusades—series of wars to capture the Holy Land, launched in 1095 by European Christians.

QUESTIONS TO CONSIDER

1. Why, after the terrorist attacks of September 11, would someone feel that "everything will be different from now on"?

2. Why might it be easier to fight an enemy that is a country rather than a "cause"?

3. Why does Professor Bacevich say that wars are about political objectives and that Americans must ask, as they respond to terrorism, what our political objectives are?

4. What does Rev. Cantwell mean when she advises her parishioners that it's okay to be "angry" at God but not "shut God out"?

5. What are some ways in which you or your friends have found your values and beliefs changed as a result of the threat of terrorism?

A Measured Response

Several vital questions faced the U.S. government after the September 11 attacks. What military actions should be taken against these terrorists? What diplomatic and economic steps should the United States take in eliminating the causes of terrorism? One of the goals for the government was to create a worldwide coalition to fight terrorism. The government tried to make September 11 stand out not as an attack on Americans, but as an attack on the democratic values and freedom found throughout the world. America's aim was also to punish the guilty without also punishing large numbers of the innocent, for that would just be a recruiting tool for a new generation of terrorists. In two newspaper articles, Kevin Danaher and Thomas L. Friedman discuss the difficulties of the U.S. response. Both articles were written in late September 2001, before the U.S. bombing of Afghanistan began, but after it seemed likely.

Justice, Not War

by Kevin Danaher

A momentous decision confronts us as a nation: Do we define the violence of Sept. 11 as an act of war or as a crime against humanity? If we define it as war, it couches the issues in nationalist sentiment and separates us from the people of other nations. If we define it as a crime against humanity, it holds the potential for uniting humankind against the scourge of terrorism.

Defining our national stance as "war" takes us more in the direction of the garrison state.[1] We are already one of the most heavily armed societies in history. Need we go further in that direction—killing innocent foreigners and restricting our own freedoms—before we realize it is the wrong direction for our country?

Rather than relying on the failed policies of the past and pushing the world into a descending **vortex**[2] of violence, we need to help people move forward to a world of justice and peace.

Much as we may want to **demonize**[3] the people who organized the mass violence of Sept. 11, we must admit that the sophistication of the attack tells us these people are capable of rational thought. If we attack indiscriminately and kill innocent people, the photos of those dead Muslims will be the greatest recruiting tool the terrorists could ask for. Do we want to strengthen their outreach capabilities among the 1 billion Muslims of the world?

The twin pillars of U.S. power in the world—money and weapons—have spawned many enemies. And now that we have been wounded, to lash out with more violence will only throw fuel on the fire. Just imagine events like those of Sept. 11 happening on a regular basis, and the warmongers calling for more and

---

[1] garrison state—nation organized primarily for war.

[2] **vortex**—situation that draws everything into itself.

[3] **demonize**—present as evil.

more retaliation as the horror escalates. If violence were capable of ending violence, we would have had a peaceful planet by now.

Instead of relying on the money values and weapons that got us into this trouble, we should rely on the greatest source of U.S. legitimacy around the world: our belief in the inherent right of all human beings to speak their minds, to assemble freely to petition government for change, to worship as they please and to participate actively in running their government. These human rights—and being the most diverse population in the world—are the pillars upon which we can rebuild U.S. credibility in the world.

Yet, if we reject the call for more violence, how do we go about the process of eliminating terrorism from the planet? First we must remember that we are not the only victims of terrorism. When terrorists massacred tourists in Egypt, that country could not declare "war" against the world. Algeria has been tormented by terrorist violence for decades, and it has not attacked other nations.

Many countries have suffered from varied terrorist acts, some perpetrated with U.S. weapons (American companies are the largest arms merchants in the world), and the people of those countries would love to end terrorism once and for all.

So let's redefine the attacks of Sept. 11 as a crime against humanity. Do we want to be seen by the world as a violent bully, mainly concerned with consuming a disproportionate share of the world's resources, or do we want to be seen as a global promoter of even-handed justice?

The perpetrators of the recent attacks can be apprehended and brought to justice without killing innocent civilians if we have the support of the world's governments. If America were to engage the world in setting up an effective international criminal court system, the support from other nations would be so strong it would be impossible for any country to shelter the perpetrators of mass violence.

Yes, a long trial exposing information on who these people are and where they learned their deadly craft would be embarrassing to some people in our government. But God help us if we are unable to criticize our public servants and rectify mistaken policies of the past.

As citizens, we cannot sit back and assume that our current policies and our current leaders will rectify the problem. We are now in uncharted waters, and the ship of state is being steered by some of the same people who got us into this mess in the first place. This is a time for the citizens of America to stand up and demand internationalism rather than isolationism, justice rather than revenge, and love rather than hate.

As the father of the Republican Party, Abraham Lincoln, once said: "The only safe way to destroy an enemy is to make him your friend."

Hama Rules

by Thomas L. Friedman

In February 1982 the secular Syrian government of President Hafez al-Assad[4] faced a mortal threat from Islamic extremists, who sought to topple the Assad regime. How did it respond? President Assad identified the rebellion as emanating from Syria's fourth-largest city—Hama—and he literally leveled it, pounding the fundamentalist neighborhoods with artillery for days. Once the guns fell silent, he plowed up the rubble and bulldozed it flat, into vast parking lots. Amnesty International[5] estimated that 10,000 to 25,000 Syrians,

---

[4] Hafez al-Assad—(1930–2000) president of Syria (1971–2000) who ruled with an iron fist, often brutally suppressing dissension. He sponsored terrorists in both Syria and Lebanon, and launched a surprise attack on Israel in 1973. He also joined the U.S.-led alliance against Iraq in the Persian Gulf War due to his bitter rivalry with Saddam Hussein.

[5] Amnesty International—organization devoted to the release of political prisoners and the attainment of human rights all over the world. It was awarded the Nobel Peace Prize in 1977.

mostly civilians, were killed in the merciless crackdown. Syria has not had a Muslim extremist problem since.

I visited Hama a few months after it was leveled. The regime actually wanted Syrians to go see it, to contemplate Hama's silence and to reflect on its meaning. I wrote afterward, "The whole town looked as though a tornado had swept back and forth over it for a week—but this was not the work of Mother Nature."

This was "Hama Rules"—the real rules of Middle East politics—and Hama Rules are no rules at all. I tell this story not to suggest this should be America's approach. We can't go around leveling cities. We need to be much more focused, selective, and smart in uprooting the terrorists.

No, I tell this story because it's important that we understand that Syria, Egypt, Algeria, and Tunisia have all faced Islamist threats and crushed them without mercy or Miranda rights.[6] Part of the problem America now faces is actually the fallout from these crackdowns.

Three things happened:

First, once the fundamentalists were crushed by the Arab states they fled to the last wild, uncontrolled places in the region—Lebanon's Bekaa Valley and Afghanistan—or to the freedom of America and Europe.

Second, some Arab regimes, most of which are corrupt dictatorships afraid of their own people, made a devil's pact with the fundamentalists. They allowed the Islamists' domestic supporters to continue raising money, ostensibly for Muslim welfare groups, and to funnel it to the Osama bin Ladens—on the condition that the Islamic extremists not attack these regimes. The Saudis in particular struck that bargain.

---

[6] Miranda rights—also known as "Miranda warnings," these are statements that the U.S. Supreme Court ruled in *Miranda v. Arizona* (1966) must be made to suspects prior to police interrogation. These guidelines, which ensure prisoners' rights and protection from unfair detention and prosecution, include informing suspects that they have the right to remain silent and the right to speak with an attorney.

Third, these Arab regimes, feeling defensive about their Islamic crackdowns, allowed their own press and intellectuals total freedom to attack America and Israel, as a way of deflecting criticism from themselves.

As a result, a generation of Muslims and Arabs have been raised on such distorted views of America that despite the fact that America gives Egypt $2 billion a year, despite the fact that America fought for the freedom of Muslims in Kuwait, Bosnia and Kosovo, and despite the fact that Bill Clinton met with Yasir Arafat more than with any other foreign leader, America has been vilified as the biggest enemy of Islam. And that is one reason that many people in the Arab-Muslim world today have either applauded the attack on America or will tell you—with a straight face—that it was all a C.I.A.-Mossad[7] plot to embarrass the Muslim world.

We need the moderate Arab states as our partners— but we don't need only their intelligence. We need them to be intelligent. I don't expect them to order their press to say nice things about America or Israel. They are entitled to their views on both, and both at times deserve criticism. But what they have never encouraged at all is for anyone to consistently present an alternative, positive view of America—even though they were sending their kids here to be educated. Anyone who did would be immediately branded a C.I.A. agent.

And while the Arab states have crushed their Islamic terrorists, they have never confronted them ideologically and delegitimized their behavior as un-Islamic. Arab and Muslim Americans are not part of this problem. But they could be an important part of the solution by engaging in the debate back in the Arab world, and presenting another vision of America.

---

[7] Mossad—most important of all intelligence agencies in Israel; Mossad's leaders report directly to the prime minister. Its agents are thought to have captured or assassinated numerous enemies of Israel, such as terrorists and former Nazis in hiding.

So America's standing in the Arab-Muslim world is now very low—partly because we have not told our story well, partly because of policies we have adopted, and partly because inept, barely legitimate Arab leaders have deliberately deflected domestic criticism of themselves onto us. The result: We must now fight a war against terrorists who are crazy and evil but who, it grieves me to say, reflect the mood in their home countries more than we might think.

QUESTIONS TO CONSIDER

1. According to Kevin Danaher, why does it matter how we define the attacks of September 11, 2001?

2. What did Abraham Lincoln mean when he said, "The only safe way to destroy an enemy is to make him your friend"?

3. What does Thomas L. Friedman mean by the phrase "Hama Rules"?

4. Why might it be hard for the United States to adopt its own set of Hama Rules?

5. How do both authors share a similar point of view?

The Media's Responsibility

Terrorism relies upon media coverage. Without journalists, this form of violence would have a very limited effect. Terrorism is a form of propaganda. Propaganda is generally defined as art or literature devoted to spreading a particular idea or belief. Some scholars have defined terrorism as "propaganda of the deed," violence designed to draw attention to a cause and to make people afraid for their own safety. The terrorism directed at Western countries would have little effect without the media. Unlike Tamil terrorism or anti-Israeli terrorism that is locally directed to force a country to give up land, terrorism against Western nations is meant to draw attention and convince the West to use its massive political and economic power to help the terrorists achieve certain ends. If this is the case, who is the media responsible to in its coverage of terrorist acts? Some people feel that the intense coverage of violence increases the likelihood of more violence. Most journalists point out, however, that they have an obligation to report the news as truth without regard to the consequences. These issues were discussed by journalist Charles Krauthammer at a 1984 symposium on media responsibility and by James Kelly in a 1986 Time magazine article about NBC's decision to interview a wanted terrorist.

Media Terrorism

by Charles Krauthammer

When we discuss terrorism we are really talking about at least three different kinds of political violence. The first and oldest kind is assassination, the usual form of political violence before World War II. The political assassin does not need the media to explain what his act means; in fact, often he does not want publicity at all. His object is simply to eliminate a political actor.

The second form of terrorism, which emerged after the war, is the random attack on civilians, but civilians of a particular type—civilians who are members of the enemy class or nationality. Terrorism of this sort, as practiced, for example, by the FLN[1] in Algeria in the late 1950s and early 1960s, is also independent of the media. Its object is to demoralize the enemy during a war, and its audience is the victim himself and his compatriots. In the case of Algeria, it was the *pieds noirs*, the French living there.

The . . . newest form of terrorism, which the PLO[2] largely created after 1968, is the random attack on anyone. We might refer to this as "media terrorism," for it can exist only if there is an interpreter to give it meaning. The terrorist acts of the PLO were not intended to demoralize the Israelis—the PLO has never really been at war with Israel—but to publicize political grievances. And the intended audience was not the immediate victims—the airline passengers—or even the Israelis, but the entire world. For such actions, coverage by the mass media becomes absolutely essential. This is where terrorists' utter dependence on the media begins.

Media terrorism—such as the 1975 murder of three Dutchmen who happened to be on a commuter train

---

[1] FLN—National Liberation Front, an Algerian group that waged a guerrilla struggle for independence from France in the period 1954–1962.

[2] PLO—Palestine Liberation Organization.

hijacked by Moluccans,[3] or the 1976 seizure of Yugoslavian hostages by Croatian[4] terrorists—is a form of political advertising. In the latter instance, the Croatians demanded that U.S. newspapers publish their **manifesto**.[5] Since the outlaws cannot buy television time, they have to earn it through terrorist acts. Like the sponsors of early television who produced shows as vehicles for their commercials, media terrorists now provide drama—murder and kidnapping, live—in return for advertising time.

The media's responsibility to act with self-restraint is obviously greatest with this kind of terrorism. In those cases where the victim is chosen at random and has no connection whatever with any political struggle, terrorism is actually a lure to attract the media. Through his acts, the terrorist tries to earn a stage on which to proclaim his message. And the media then take upon themselves the duty of interpreting those acts. In 1979, for example, terrorists attacked the American Embassy in Beirut with grenades. One network correspondent explained that this action was "perhaps an expression of resentment and frustration" on the part of Palestinians over the Israeli-Egyptian peace treaty. Here we reach a level where an attack on innocents is rationalized as a psychological necessity. Or consider the attack on a bus near Tel Aviv last April: it was generally explained as the PLO's assertion that it still existed after its expulsion from Lebanon, a kind of "I kill, therefore I am." Without the press to carry this message, the act would have been meaningless; in fact, since it had no military or political purpose, it probably would not have been committed in

---

[3] Moluccans—inhabitants of more than 1,000 islands in eastern Indonesia, formerly a Dutch colony.

[4] Croatian—belonging to the independent nation of Croatia in what was formerly unified Yugoslavia.

[5] **manifesto**—public declaration of principles, policies, or intentions, especially those of a political nature.

the first place. I believe that when the point of a terrorist attack is to force the media to function as interpreters, the media have a heavy responsibility not to do the interpreting. . . .

There can be no question that the development of enormously powerful communications technology, and the fact that this technology is in the hands of people who believe in competing with one another to get a good story, have produced a new phenomenon. The American hostages[6] would not have been held so long had the Iranians not realized that they had created the most effective television stage in history, which gave them immediate access to millions of people. The Iranians exploited the hostage crisis in a way that they could not have done in the absence of television cameras.

Now, I want to give an example of the sort of media self-restraint that I am suggesting. In the late 1970s, there was a rash of episodes in which spectators at sporting events jumped out onto the playing field for their fifteen seconds of exposure on national television. After a number of these episodes, some of the networks decided to turn the cameras away. Instead, a reporter would say, "There's someone running out onto the field, but we won't show him to you because if we do, it will encourage other clowns to do the same thing." Now, when you hear the crowd cheering as the clowns are being chased off the field, you really want to see what is happening. But clearly it is worth forgoing that pleasure in order to gain a greater societal good—the nondisruption of future ball games. I think media executives should exercise the same self-restraint in covering terrorism, when the societal good to be gained is reducing the incentive to political murder.

---

[6] American hostages—On November 4, 1979, radical Iranian students seized the U.S. embassy in Tehran, taking 52 Americans hostage. The crisis continued until January 20, 1981, when the hostages were released.

Caught by the Camera
by James Kelly

The man on the screen seemed distinctly ill at ease. Puffing on Marlboros, his eyes darting nervously between camera and interviewer, he vowed to launch terrorist attacks against Americans at home and abroad. That was not all; he labeled Ronald Reagan "enemy No. 1," implying that the President of the U.S. is a prime target for assassination.

Until last week, Americans had seen Mohammed Abul Abbas Zaidan, better known as Abul Abbas, only in a few still photographs and snippets of TV footage. The accused plotter behind last fall's hijacking of the *Achille Lauro*[7] and hence a suspect in the murder of cruise ship passenger Leon Klinghoffer, Abbas is on most-wanted lists in the U.S., Italy and Israel. Suddenly, however, the elusive Palestinian showed up on American television last week. In exchange for the exclusive 3-minute interview, NBC News executives agreed not to disclose Abbas' whereabouts, an arrangement that stirred up almost as much debate among U.S. officials and journalists as the larger issue of whether a hardened terrorist like Abbas should be allowed to use American television as a platform to air his deadly views.

"Obviously, terrorism thrives on this kind of publicity," said Charles Redman, a State Department spokesman. Robert Oakley, head of the State Department's counterterrorism office, called NBC's decision to keep Abbas' location secret **"reprehensible"**[8] and accused the network of becoming, in effect, the terrorist's "accomplice."

There is nothing novel about a news organization acceding to ground rules in pursuit of a story, and that

---

[7] *Achille Lauro*—Italian cruise ship hijacked in 1985 by members of the Palestine Liberation Front under the leadership of Abul Abbas. After a passenger was killed, Abbas became one of the most wanted terrorists in the world.

[8] **reprehensible**—blameworthy.

includes pledging not to disclose details of where interviews took place. Most reporters also seem to shy away from any definitive prohibition on interviewing fugitives, even those wanted for murder. "We as journalists don't see ourselves as an extension of any law-enforcement agency," says John Seigenthaler, editorial page editor of *USA Today*. "What the journalist has to consider is whether the information to be gained is so vital that it tips the scale in favor of granting protection to a fugitive."

In the view of many editors, including Seigenthaler, the Abbas interview did not pass that test. Abbas uttered only predictable propaganda, offering little that was new or surprising. "I didn't see anything that was remarkable or enlightening," says George Cotliar, managing editor of the *Los Angeles Times*. Comments Karen Elliott House, foreign editor of the *Wall Street Journal*: "We are not in the business of spreading propaganda but in the business of analyzing why things happen and what they mean. I don't see [the interview] as a great journalistic coup."

Some journalists criticized NBC not so much for conducting an interview with a wanted terrorist as for agreeing to give up the most newsworthy element of the story. Warren Hoge, foreign editor of the *New York Times*, says that his paper was offered an Abbas interview several weeks after the ship hijacking, but turned it down. "We can't agree to an arrangement where we can't publish the single most important fact, which is [Abbas's] whereabouts," says Hoge. *Chicago Tribune* editor James Squires was so incensed by the NBC deal that he wrote his paper's editorial denouncing it. "They missed the news," says Squires. "We're in the news business and the news is 'Where is Abbas?'" (Though the U.S. Government refused to speculate, Italian authorities last week said the terrorist was in Tunisia[9] and an **extradition**[10] request has been made.)

Several terrorism experts and lawmakers argued that the NBC interview only plays into the hands of terrorists, providing a media spotlight that a man like Abbas needs to dramatize his cause. Indeed, Abbas received extraordinary mileage out of his appearance. Asked at the Tokyo summit about the implied threat against his life, Reagan said, "Let him try," thus elevating a terrorist's bark to something worthy of a presidential response in front of hundreds of reporters from around the world.

Some journalists endorsed NBC's decision. Charles Lewis, Washington bureau chief of the Associated Press, argues that Abbas' "enormous mystery" made the interview worth doing. Ed Turner, executive vice president of CNN, says, "We would have run it. There's no question that Abbas is a major news figure, for good or for ill."

NBC News President Lawrence Grossman says there was no debate within the network over whether to agree to Abbas' secrecy request. "It's critical that people know about terrorist leaders and what their plans are and what they are like," says Grossman. According to correspondent Henry Champ, it took two months for NBC to make contact with Abbas and secure his consent; other than asking that his location not be revealed, Abbas set no conditions for the interview, which took place two weeks ago.

The Abbas incident is not likely to inspire news organizations to write fresh guidelines about interviewing terrorists or cutting deals with fugitives. Such rules can never cover all possible **contingencies**[11] anyway.

---

[9] Tunisia—country in northern Africa bordering the Mediterranean Sea.

[10] **extradition**—legal surrender of a fugitive to the jurisdiction of another state, country, or government for trial.

[11] **contingencies**—events that may occur but are not likely or intended; possibilities.

Nonetheless, greater care should be exercised to ensure that a terrorist does not use the interview simply for his own means. If correspondent Champ asked tough, probing questions of Abbas—about the murder of passenger Klinghoffer, for example—the televised excerpts did not reflect it. NBC may have won a scoop, but it lost the larger battle for first-rate journalism.

QUESTIONS TO CONSIDER

1. What is "media terrorism" and how is it different from other forms?

2. What did Charles Krauthammer mean when he said the media sometimes acts as "interpreters" of terrorist acts?

3. Why might avoiding giving publicity to terrorists be more difficult than avoiding showing the fan who disrupts a sporting event?

4. Why was NBC criticized for broadcasting the interview with Abbas?

5. How does the incident described in "Caught by the Camera" present the problem the media must face in covering terrorism?

6. In your opinion, what are the media's responsibilities when it comes to terrorism?

The Price of Security

Another of the important post-September 11 debates in the United States was about how the measures the government takes to safeguard Americans from terrorist attack would affect personal liberty. Immediately after the attack a bill was put forward in Congress to increase the government's ability to investigate, detain, and deport suspects in an effort to prevent terrorism, not just catch those responsible after the act. But there was a great deal of worry that government efforts to stop terrorism would go too far. National identity cards were proposed, as were the monitoring and storage of e-mails, and the creation of harsher laws to detain and deport immigrants. For most Americans, the goal is to not make the cure for terrorism worse than the illness. Journalist Richard Lacayo wrote editorials for Time *magazine commenting on both an earlier anti-terrorism bill proposed after the Oklahoma City bombing in 1995 and on the 2001 bill. Senator Russ Feingold discussed the 2001 bill at Senate hearings on this legislation.*

Rushing to Bash Outsiders

by Richard Lacayo

For a while last week, something in the national mood appeared to be turning darkly against Arab Americans—at least for as long as it was supposed that

the Oklahoma blast might be the work of Islamic terrorists. In a replay of the harassment they suffered during
the Gulf War, mosques reported receiving telephone
threats. On *Larry King Live*, former Oklahoma
Congressman Dave McCurdy pointed to an Islamic conference, full of fire-breathing rhetoric, that was held in
Oklahoma City in 1992. That was one reason, he said,
that he knew terrorism "could happen here."

When it emerged that the first serious suspects in the
bombing were not Arabs or Muslims, the threat of a
backlash subsided. What did not change was the sudden
momentum behind passage of an antiterrorism bill
bitterly opposed by many Arab-American groups, as
well as civil libertarians.[1] On Capitol Hill, where the
members of Congress are eager to show that they are
doing something to prevent future outrages, the
omnibus counterterrorism act of 1995 is now getting
serious attention. Proposed by the Clinton
Administration in the wake of the World Trade Center
bombing, it would, among its many provisions, crack
down on fund-raising activities in the U.S. that benefit
organizations identified as terrorist and make some
deportations easier. Though it was introduced in
February and had bipartisan support—many of its ideas
were first broached by Republican administrations—the
bill was a low-profile initiative until the bombing.
Within a day it had become a top priority, with Senate
majority leader Bob Dole promising quick action.

"It will seriously erode civil liberties," complains
James Zogby, president of the Arab American Institute. "I
think it would be terrible if the legislation passed in this
atmosphere." One provision that has angered the bill's
opponents would permit the deportation of aliens who
donate money to activities sponsored by groups that the

---

[1] civil libertarians—those who are actively concerned with the protection of
those rights guaranteed to the individual by law.

President has determined are involved in terrorism, even if the money was earmarked for ostensibly peaceful purposes, such as schools or medical assistance. That could affect fund-raising in the U.S. on behalf of nonviolent undertakings by Arab groups that also have paramilitary wings. That, says the American Civil Liberties Union,[2] would be a violation of the First Amendment right of association.

Another part of the bill would change the rules for deportation hearings against aliens suspected of being linked to terrorists. It would allow the government to use evidence that it would not have to divulge in detail to the accused; only a government "summary" would be provided. Law-enforcement agencies want the rule change as a way to protect the identity of informers and government infiltrators who provide information. "It would set a dangerous precedent," says Charles Wheeler, director of the National Immigration Law Center in Los Angeles. "If they can [proceed against] foreigners based on secret information, they could do it to citizens."

Even one of the bill's sponsors in the Senate, Democrat Joe Biden of Delaware, disavowed the evidence provision, calling it "Kafkaesque."[3] But by last week Biden was predicting that compromise language would be worked out. Charles Schumer, the New York Democrat who sponsored the bill in the House, insists that the summary hearings would apply to a "very limited number of cases."

One reason pressure for the bill is likely to remain high is the ongoing trial in New York of Sheik Omar

---

[2] American Civil Liberties Union—organization founded in 1920 to protect Americans' constitutional rights and freedoms.

[3] Kafkaesque—reference to the nightmarish quality found in the writings of Franz Kafka (1883–1924); his work expresses anxieties about modern life and often features bureaucratic terror, lack of justice, and a nonsensical legal system.

Abdel Rahman.[4] He and 11 others have been accused of plotting to blow up the U.N. and a federal office building, as well as a bridge and two tunnels that connect Manhattan to New Jersey. In the second week of the trial, one of Rahman's co-defendants unexpectedly changed his plea to guilty and claimed that the sheik had offered the approval of Islamic law for the terror campaign. If the Administration's bill had been in place, it might have made it easier to expel Rahman and his associates. As for the Oklahoma bombing, if it was indeed entirely the work of Americans, Washington's new weapon against terrorism may be pointed in the wrong direction.

Terrorizing Ourselves
by Richard Lacayo

Emergencies have always been a time when the niceties of law have been most vulnerable to the demands of national security or national hysteria. As Senate minority leader Trent Lott said last week, "When you're in this type of conflict, when you're at war, civil liberties are treated differently." World War II produced the internment camps for Japanese Americans, a development upheld in 1944 by the Supreme Court but later repudiated. After the bombing at the federal building in Oklahoma City, the Immigration and Naturalization Service was authorized to establish a new court to consider the deportation of suspected alien terrorists, in which cases would be heard without the usual obligation to inform the accused of the evidence against them.

Now the Bush Administration is considering the establishment of special military **tribunals**.[5] Suspected

---

[4] Omar Abdel Rahman—Muslim cleric from Egypt who in 1996 was convicted of waging "a war of urban terrorism" against the United States. He had plans to bomb prominent sites in New York City such as the United Nations and to assassinate leaders such as President Mubarak of Egypt. Rahman was also found guilty in the 1990 murder of Rabbi Meir Kahane.

[5] **tribunals**—courts of justice or committees or boards appointed to judge in a particular matter.

terrorists could be tried without the ordinary legal constraints of American justice. During World War II, German **saboteurs**[6] were tried secretly that way in Washington, and those convicted were hanged 30 days later.

Just one day after last week's attacks, the Senate also approved a provision expanding the circumstances under which law-enforcement agencies can force Internet service providers to hand over information about subscriber e-mails. If the Federal government were to monitor more e-mails, a key question would be whether it would hold on to them for some time or dispose of them almost at once, as it now does with the information obtained from instant background checks mandated by federal law for gun purchases. Americans may be willing to let their e-mails pass one time through a sort of national filter that would screen for hints of terrorist activity. They will be far more reluctant to allow the government to collect a national e-mail database.

Civil libertarians expect renewed calls for a national identification card. The cards could have photographs and hard-to-falsify identifying information like handprint or retina data that could be read by scanners at, say, airline counters. If cards were required for many common transactions—renting a car, buying an airline ticket—they would be useful for keeping track of criminals and terrorists. Or you. Eva Jefferson Paterson, executive director of the Lawyers' Committee on Civil Rights Under Law in San Francisco, predicts that innocent citizens would be challenged constantly to produce their cards. "You could be stopped by the police to prove you can walk down the street," she says. "Poor people and people of color would be stopped the most."

There could also be stepped-up public surveillance. At last year's Super Bowl in Tampa, Fla., law-enforcement officials secretly scanned spectators' faces with

---

[6] **saboteurs**—those who commit sabotage, or the destruction of property or obstruction of normal operations, usually in time of war.

surveillance cameras and instantly matched their face prints against photographs of suspected terrorists and known criminals in computerized databases. Facial-recognition technology might help, says Bruce Hoffman, vice president for external affairs at the Rand Corp. and a former adviser to the National Commission on Terrorism, but mostly after the fact, during an investigation. And that means storing all the face data collected, something civil libertarians fear will allow the government to track any individual. If systems were set up all over a city, you could be "check pointed" by camera when you board a train, stop at a cash machine and enter a store or the place where you work. "We are vulnerable," says Hoffman, "and there's a certain level of risk that we have to accept and live with. To me, the cure can be far worse than the disease."

Says Morton Halperin, senior fellow at the Council on Foreign Relations: "If you take both security and civil liberties seriously, you can find solutions that respect individual rights and privacy and still give the intelligence and law enforcement agencies the scope that they need. We had worked that out in terms of airports. Nobody thinks you have the civil liberty to take knives on airplanes. I don't know who made the decision to let people bring knives on anyway, but it was certainly not civil libertarians."

Statement on Anti-Terrorism Bill
by Senator Russ Feingold

Mr. President, I have asked for this time to speak about the antiterrorism bill before us, H.R. 3162. As we address this bill, we are especially mindful of the terrible events of September 11 and beyond, which led to the bill's proposal and its quick consideration in the Congress.

I believe we must redouble our vigilance. We must redouble our vigilance to ensure our security and to prevent further acts of terror. But we must also redouble our vigilance to preserve our values and the basic rights that make us who we are.

The Founders who wrote our Constitution and Bill of Rights[7] exercised that vigilance even though they had recently fought and won the Revolutionary War. They did not live in comfortable and easy times of hypothetical enemies. They wrote a Constitution of limited powers and an explicit Bill of Rights to protect liberty in times of war, as well as in times of peace.

There have been periods in our nation's history when civil liberties have taken a backseat to what appeared at the time to be the legitimate **exigencies**[8] of war. Our national consciousness still bears the stain and the scars of those events: The Alien and Sedition Acts,[9] the suspension of habeas corpus[10] during the Civil War, the internment of Japanese Americans, German Americans, and Italian Americans during World War II, the blacklisting[11] of supposed communist sympathizers during the McCarthy era,[12] and the **surveillance**[13] and harassment of antiwar protesters, including Dr. Martin Luther King, Jr., during the Vietnam War. We must not allow these pieces of our past to become prologue.

---

[7] Bill of Rights—first ten amendments to the U.S. Constitution, added in 1791 and consisting of a formal list of citizens' rights and freedoms.

[8] **exigencies**—urgent situations.

[9] Alien and Sedition Acts—series of four laws enacted in 1798 to reduce the political power of recent immigrants to the United States.

[10] habeas corpus—document requiring that a prisoner be brought before a court or judge so that it can be decided whether his or her imprisonment is legal.

[11] blacklisting—Hollywood's policy in the late 1940s and early 1950s of refusing to hire creative artists, such as writers and directors, because of their suspected ties to communists. Hundreds of people were fired, and many were never able to work in the movie industry again.

[12] McCarthy era—period from 1950 until 1954 during which Senator Joseph McCarthy (1908–1957) led an influential and feared campaign against communists and their supporters within the U.S. government despite his inability to make a convincing case against any of the accused.

[13] **surveillance**—close observation of a person or group, especially one under suspicion.

Now some may say, indeed we may hope, that we have come a long way since those days of infringements on civil liberties. But there is ample reason for concern. And I have been troubled in the past six weeks by the potential loss of commitment in the Congress and the country to traditional civil liberties.

As it seeks to combat terrorism, the Justice Department is making extraordinary use of its power to arrest and detain individuals, jailing hundreds of people on immigration violations and arresting more than a dozen "material witnesses" not charged with any crime. Although the government has used these authorities before, it has not done so on such a broad scale. Judging from government announcements, the government has not brought any criminal charges related to the attacks with regard to the overwhelming majority of these detainees.

For example, the FBI arrested as a material witness the San Antonio radiologist Albader Al-Hazmi, who has a name like two of the hijackers, and who tried to book a flight to San Diego for a medical conference. According to his lawyer, the government held Al-Hazmi incommunicado after his arrest, and it took six days for lawyers to get access to him. After the FBI released him, his lawyer said, "This is a good lesson about how frail our processes are. It's how we treat people in difficult times like these that is the true test of the democracy and civil liberties that we brag so much about throughout the world." I agree with those statements.

Now, it so happens that since early 1999, I have been working on another bill that is poignantly relevant to recent events: legislation to prohibit racial profiling, especially the practice of targeting pedestrians or drivers for stops and searches based on the color of their skin. Before September 11th, people spoke of the issue mostly in the context of African Americans and

Latino Americans who had been profiled. But after September 11, the issue has taken on a new context and a new urgency.

Even as America addresses the demanding security challenges before us, we must strive mightily also to guard our values and basic rights. We must guard against racism and ethnic discrimination against people of Arab and South Asian origin and those who are Muslim.

Of course, there is no doubt that if we lived in a police state, it would be easier to catch terrorists. If we lived in a country that allowed the police to search your home at any time for any reason; if we lived in a country that allowed the government to open your mail, eavesdrop on your phone conversations, or intercept your e-mail communications; if we lived in a country that allowed the government to hold people in jail indefinitely based on what they write or think, or based on mere suspicion that they are up to no good, then the government would no doubt discover and arrest more terrorists.

But that probably would not be a country in which we would want to live. And that would not be a country for which we could, in good conscience, ask our young people to fight and die. In short, that would not be America.

Preserving our freedom is one of the main reasons that we are now engaged in this new war on terrorism. We will lose that war without firing a shot if we sacrifice the liberties of the American people.

That is why I found the anti-terrorism bill originally proposed by Attorney General Ashcroft and President Bush to be troubling.

QUESTIONS TO CONSIDER

1. How are the themes and arguments of Richard Lacayo's two editorials, written six years apart, similar to each other?

2. What are some arguments that could be used for and against the adoption of a national identification card?

3. Why might Senator Feingold feel anxious about criticizing the president's proposed anti-terrorism bill?

4. Why does Feingold mention the times in which the writers of the Constitution lived?

5. What does Feingold mean when he says that the United States is in danger of losing the war on terrorism "without firing a shot"?

6. Under what conditions would it be acceptable to put up with some decrease in civil liberties in order to achieve more security? Explain your answer.

The Need for Tolerance

One of the constant themes of American leaders after the
September 11 attacks was the need to avoid blaming Arab-Americans.
There are over 3 million Arab-Americans, and President Bush
worked hard to remind the country that we are all Americans, no
matter where we come from, no matter where we worship. One of
America's strengths is its diversity. It is obvious that all Americans
were attacked on September 11, not just one racial group or one
religious group. Still, after the attacks, people who looked Middle
Eastern were pulled off airplanes, insulted, even in a small number
of cases assaulted. Richard Rothstein's essay in The New York
Times and a letter to the editor of that newspaper by an Indian-
American woman both address the need for tolerance.

The Other War, Against Intolerance
by Richard Rothstein

PROVIDENCE, R.I.—The day after the attacks,
an Amtrak train was detained here, and police officers
seized a bearded man wearing a turban, suspecting him

of **complicity**.[1] The authorities cordoned off downtown, disrupting commuters' and students' travel home. The city's Muslim minority feared hostility and repression.

The next morning Zozan Haji, 15, one of six children in a family of Kurdish refugees from Iraq, removed the Muslim head scarf she had always worn. But her quest to blend in was unsuccessful. As Zozan walked into Feinstein High School, three African-American boys threatened to attack her.

What happened next may not be typical. But as the nation debates how to balance security with civil liberties, how much emphasis to give to defense, to **retribution**,[2] to prevention, the focus of many schools in the last two decades on multiculturalism and conflict resolution may make it less likely for rash views to prevail.

After Zozan reported the threats, Nancy Owen, the principal, spoke with her, and with the boys and their parents. She summoned district psychologists to lead school-wide assemblies the next morning, followed by small-group discussions.

In these groups, some boys—many of them African-American, though not all—told how angered they were at being singled out themselves, profiled by the police. Some of these boys had empathy for Zozan. But not all of them did. More often, the greatest insistence that pro-filing Muslims is wrong came from African-American girls, though their experience with police hostility is less direct.

In each group, teachers reminded students about their studies of the many cultures that make up this nation. Literacy instruction in elementary schools, for example, now often uses readings from the works of not only white authors but also ethnic minorities—African-Americans, Native Americans, Asian-Americans, Hispanics—to help pupils identify with characters from each.

---

[1] **complicity**—involvement.

[2] **retribution**—punishment.

The district's high school history textbook calls racial, ethnic and religious diversity the nation's most compelling theme, saying this is sometimes a strength, sometimes a challenge. "The United States," the text states, "has struggled with contradictory ideals concerning immigrants: the wish to promote cultural diversity and the desire to Americanize each new wave."

Nationwide, instruction that underscores the country's ethnic variety has been controversial. Critics note that students are more likely to know about Japanese-American internment during World War II than about lend-lease or Yalta. A decade ago, as schools furthered an emphasis on the nation's many ethnicities, Arthur Schlesinger, Jr., wrote a rebuke, saying such teaching would prevent children from gaining "the unifying vision of individuals from all nations melted into a new race."

At least from events at Feinstein in the last two weeks, that fear seems overblown. Even if teaching sometimes tilts too far to a focus on Americans' diverse origins, students who are most proud of their own ancestry have not become those who are least tolerant of others. Rather, those rushing most strongly to Zozan's defense were students who correlated her experiences with those of their own families and ancestors. These fiercely *American* students insist that respect for due process, individual rights and cultural difference is the unifying vision.

Other teaching has also had an effect. Many adolescents have had some instruction in conflict resolution. Again, it is African-American girls who seem to take it most seriously at Feinstein. One of them, Christine Gomes, urges military restraint. "In class," she argued, "they keep on saying that the bigger person is the one who walks away from a fight, the one who wants peace. How many people do we have to kill to make Americans feel better? Some of these politicians who want war are acting younger than we are."

Of course, such views are not universal here, and this school may not be typical. Adolescent absolutism,[3] opposed to all ethnic profiling or a war of retaliation, cannot solve the complex problems facing American leaders. The man taken off the train in Providence was singled out for his appearance and had no association with terrorists. But young Arab men are more likely than others to be part of Osama bin Laden's network. With lives at stake, do we really want to tell the police that they cannot take this into account?

Confronting difficult decisions, the nation may be stronger because many educators have cleansed curriculums of **jingoism**[4] and infused them with tolerance. As young people with such schooling participate in democratic debate, they too will find it hard to come up with answers to our national plight. But answers they develop stand an increased chance of being good ones.

Letter to the Editor

On Oct. 9, I took a flight from Dulles Airport to Newark, and security was tighter than I've ever seen it. As I was boarding the flight, I was pulled aside, along with two other men who looked Middle Eastern or Indian, during a security check. All the other passengers were allowed to board.

While I welcome the increased security at the airports and didn't mind being searched, I want people to remember that not everyone who has brown skin is a terrorist.

Perhaps everyone should be checked, or at least randomly checked. As I boarded that flight, I thought that the terrorists took away not only my freedom to fly safely but also my freedom to be me, an Indian-American born and raised in the United States.

---

[3] absolutism—single-mindedness.

[4] **jingoism**—extreme nationalism.

QUESTIONS TO CONSIDER

1. If you noticed an incident taking place like the one at Feinstein High School, how would you react?

2. Why does the district's history book call America's diversity of people its "most compelling theme"?

3. How would you answer Rothstein when he asks whether, with lives at stake, we really want to tell the police how to do their job?

4. How was the letter-writer's experience following the September 11 attacks similar to incidents mentioned by Richard Rothstein?

5. What does the letter-writer mean when she writes that the terrorists took away "my freedom to be me"?

The Real Face of Islam

BY LAURIE GOODSTEIN

There is a common tendency in the Western media and entertainment industry to present all terrorists as Muslim fanatics. But a majority of the world's Muslims believe terrorism is wrong and not at all reconcilable with their faith. Although the Quran, Islam's holy book, does call on all good Muslims to fight non-Muslims and promises them heavenly rewards, it also forbids suicide; forbids the killing of women, children, and the elderly; and insists that Islam's enemies must be fought openly, "beard to beard." In the aftermath of the World Trade Center attack, a fatwa (Arabic, "religious ruling") was issued that condemned the attack and told American Muslims that it was okay to fight on America's side in this war—the Quran explicitly forbids fighting other Muslims. An October 2001 article from The New York Times *relates the story behind this fatwa.*

A panel of prominent Muslim scholars in the Middle East has issued a fatwa, or religious opinion, denouncing the terrorist attacks on the United States and saying it is the "duty" of Muslims to participate in the mission to apprehend the terrorists.

The primary purpose of the fatwa, released at a news conference yesterday in Washington, is to reassure Muslim soldiers in the American armed forces that they are permitted to fight other Muslims and Muslim countries to combat terrorism.

The fatwa was issued in response to a request by Capt. Abdul-Rasheed Muhammad, a Muslim chaplain in the United States Army, who sought guidance for Muslim military personnel uneasy about being deployed in the operation against Afghanistan.

But several Muslim experts said the fatwa could have a broad impact beyond the United States by providing religious justification for Muslim nations to cooperate with the American military effort. Many Muslim countries have minimized the American presence within their borders or over their skies.

Fatwas are not binding, but this one is likely to have strong credibility throughout the Islamic world because among its five authors is a prominent scholar based in Qatar[1] whose word is revered by many Muslims, both moderates and militants.

That scholar, Sheik Yusuf al-Qaradawi, is regarded as an independent voice, unlike the many Islamic muftis[2] and theologians who have been appointed by some Muslim governments. Far from pro-Western, Sheik Qaradawi has been a spiritual advisor to Muslim Brotherhood militants in Egypt, has harshly criticized the United States for supporting Israel and has condoned Palestinian suicide bombers.

"This fatwa is very significant. Yusuf Qaradawi is probably the most well-known legal authority in the whole Muslim world today," said Imam Feisal Abdul Rauf, founder of the American Sufi Muslim Association, and an authority in Islamic jurisprudence. "The armed

---

[1] Qatar—country of eastern Arabia on the Persian Gulf.

[2] muftis—Muslim scholars who interpret the sharia, the Islamic law codes based on the Quran.

forces of other countries now have behind them a legal standing in the eyes of a noted legal authority to be part of the coalition against terrorism."

The fatwa, written in Arabic and translated into four pages of English, says: "We find it necessary to apprehend the true perpetrators of these crimes, as well as those who aid and abet them through incitement, financing or other support. They must be brought to justice in an impartial court of law and we must punish them appropriately, so that it could act as a deterrent to them and others like them who easily slay the lives of innocents, destroy properties and terrorize people. Hence, it is a duty on Muslims to participate in this effort with all possible means."

The fatwa condemns the terrorist attack, saying that "all Muslims ought to be united against all those who terrorize innocents," because the death of noncombatants is a clear violation of Islamic law.

The fatwa notes that American military action may also result in the death of innocent people, but that a Muslim soldier must "perform his duty in this fight despite the feeling of uneasiness of 'fighting without discriminating.'" As a soldier, "he has no choice but to follow orders, otherwise his allegiance and loyalty to his country could be in doubt."

The fatwa was issued on Sept. 27 but not released until yesterday because it was being shown to other Muslim jurists in this country and overseas, said Dr. Taha Jabir Alalwani, chairman of the Fiqh Council of North America, a group of Muslim scholars.

The fatwa is surprising because it appears to contradict other recent statements from Mr. Qaradawi.

In an interview on Sept. 16, on Al Jazeera television, the Arabic-language network based in Qatar, Mr. Qaradawi said, "A Muslim is forbidden from entering into an alliance with a non-Muslim against another Muslim." He called on Muslims to "fight the American military if we can, and if we cannot we should fight the U.S. economically and politically."

It is not clear why Mr. Qaradawi has appeared to change his position.

The other authors of the fatwa include Haytham al-Khayyat, a scholar in Syria, and three Egyptian scholars who have also criticized American policy in Muslim countries: Tariq al-Bishri, a retired jurist, Muhammad S. al-Awa, a professor of law, and Fahmi Houaydi, a newspaper columnist.

It is too early to tell how the fatwa will be greeted in either the Muslim world, or among Muslims in the United States. Fatwas can be disseminated through speeches in mosques, Web sites and media coverage.

Not everyone welcomed this fatwa. Qaseem A. Uqdah, executive director of the American Muslim Armed Forces and Veterans Affairs Council, said he was outraged that such a fatwa was even sought.

Mr. Uqdah said the fatwa was a political statement of no help to enlisted Muslims, and should never have been sought because the scholars could have come to a completely different conclusion.

"Now you have opened a door for people to question, is that right or wrong," he said. "You'll have controversy looming about us just when we don't need that."

QUESTIONS TO CONSIDER

1. What are *fatwas*, and why might they be important in the struggle against terrorism?

2. Why is the *fatwa* mentioned in the article expected to have "strong credibility" in the Muslim community?

3. Why might Muslims in the American community have conflicting feelings about their duties?

4. In your opinion, when should leaders of any religion take a stand on a political situation?

Fear and Bioterrorism

BY JARED DIAMOND

One of the main goals of most terrorists is to frighten ordinary citizens. This aspect of terrorism was evident in the weeks that followed the September 11 attacks, as a deadly strain of anthrax, a lethal bacterium, was mailed to various offices in the United States. The anthrax scare was real and widespread. Real because anthrax is extremely deadly and quickly caused the deaths of several Americans. Widespread because the attacks played to Americans' greatest fear: an undetected, deadly, and spreading enemy. The government did its best to reassure Americans, acquire enough antibiotics, and limit the effectiveness of the attack. Nonetheless, fear spread. It is the natural response, yet also the one that terrorists aim for. As U.S. President Franklin Roosevelt said to the nation during the Depression, "The only thing we have to fear is fear itself." In the following article from The New York Times, *historian Jared Diamond compares and contrasts various attacks in history aimed at civilian populations and cautions us that the only response in the face of possible death is refusal to surrender to panic.*

The essence of terrorism is to kill or injure opponents in ways specifically designed to cause fear, and thus to disorganize the opposing society to a degree far out of proportion to the number of victims. Whether this strategy is used in wartime or against a nation at peace, the desired effect is the same. The German V-1 flying bombs and V-2 rockets launched against London in 1944 killed civilians in each attack, but their psychological effect on the population was far greater than the number of dead might suggest.

We Americans are now experiencing terrorism for the first time on American soil, as well as forms of terrorism new in world history. But the phenomenon of terrorism itself is ancient. What can we learn from the past that could help us cope?

We often suppose that it was the 20th century that introduced terrorism as a conscious tactic of war. It's true that bombing of civilians in World War II to break their morale elevated military terrorism to new technological heights. Yet low-tech military terrorism has been with us since the recorded origins of war, as illustrated by Pizarro's conquistadores' chopping arms off Inca soldiers and the Spartans' murder of their Plataean prisoners, described 2,400 years ago by Thucydides.[1] Apart from such wartime terrorism, terrorist raids by neighboring tribes were a **chronic**[2] act of traditional life for New Guinea highlanders—much as terrorist attacks have persisted against Israel for decades.

Among societies targeted by terrorists, some cracked under the stress but others didn't. For instance, much to the surprise and disappointment of those bombing them, Londoners and German and Japanese city-dwellers did not crack during World War II. What explains that varying impact of terrorism? I can **discern**[3]

---

[1] Thucydides—(c. 460–c. 400 B.C.) Greek historian of the Peloponnesian War.

[2] **chronic**—habitual.

[3] **discern**—detect.

at least three factors: novelty, sense of helplessness and lack of warning.

New forms of terrorism are most frightening in their first use, when the targeted society is unprepared psychologically as well as physically. This was true for the first use of chlorine gas in World War I, the first use of nerve gas in the Iraq-Iran war, and the introduction of smallpox into the New World by Europeans and their American descendants—inadvertently to the Aztecs and intentionally to some North American Indian tribes.

Targets of terrorism tend to become most demoralized when their society appears to be helpless to protect them. Like terrorism itself, countermeasures against it have a psychological value far out of proportion to their effectiveness. For instance, on Sept. 10, 1940, when British anti-aircraft guns were first fired against the German bombers that had begun nightly raids on London on Sept. 7, their big roar gave an enormous boost to the morale of Londoners even though they hit only a few German planes.

Terrorist attacks that cannot be seen or heard coming are more damaging to morale than those detectable before arrival. A lack of warning means that a possible attack must be feared constantly.

Civilians in World War II did not crack under bombing attacks for several reasons. Over time, the attacks lost their novelty. The bombers were seen to be met by anti-aircraft fire and defending fighters. And bombs other than German V-2 rockets were delivered noisily or visibly, allowing civilians to prepare for attack.

What has just happened to us in recent weeks is awful beyond anything that we have experienced previously. That makes it all the more important to understand events since Sept. 11 in full context.

Before Sept. 11, we assumed that we were protected by the oceans and our nuclear arsenal. Without warning, we were catapulted in a single day from peace to a terrorist war and then to bioterrorism within a month. The telescoping of our experience in this war, with its forms of terrorism unprecedented anywhere, is what makes the events of the past several weeks so incomprehensible and nightmarish.

Other novel forms of terrorism probably await us, but a future attack can no longer shock us: in fact, the possibility of attack is now a main focus of attention in the press and in conversation. While the first hijacked suicide planes and anthrax envelopes arrived without warning, we have already learned to see our world differently, scrutinizing unexpected envelopes and airline passengers for potential weapons. Although the effectiveness of these first countermeasures may be like that of London's first anti-aircraft barrage (few hits but a lot of noise), their sophistication and therefore effectiveness will increase with time. Though we may feel vulnerable, the United States is better able to devise and deploy countermeasures, whether against skyjacking or anthrax or any still-to-be-deployed threat, than any other nation in history.

The current crop of terrorists, unlike the bombers of World War II, has no chance of conquering us or (realistically) of killing a large fraction of our population. They cannot destroy us; our biggest risk is our own panic. What we face is terrorism in the most elementary sense: actions whose hoped-for impact is paralysis of the target rather than direct damage from the action itself. We cannot appease these terrorists or surrender to them, any more than Londoners could give in under the Blitz.[4] We will track them down, because we are much stronger than they and we have no other choice.

---

[4] Blitz—German aerial bombardment of England during World War II.

QUESTIONS TO CONSIDER

1. What are some examples of terrorism prior to the 20th century?

2. What are the three factors that explain the degree of terrorism's effect on a society?

3. According to the author, what is the best way that people can respond emotionally to terrorist attacks?

4. How is the anthrax scare similar to and different from the bombing of London during World War II?

5. What does Diamond see as our biggest risk? What is your opinion of his view?

Pursuing Terrorists

▲
Department of Alcohol, Tobacco, and Firearms officials search for clues from the 1995 bombing of the Oklahoma City federal building.

▲
The Pan Am Boeing 747 destroyed in 1988 over Lockerbie,
Scotland, is rebuilt to aid in the investigation of the disaster.

A member of the Omagh Metropolitan Police investigation team
in Northern Ireland examines fragments of rubble collected
from the 1998 bomb blast scene. ▶

MURDER
Omagh-Saturday 15th August 1998

Were you in Omagh on Saturday 15th August 1998?

Did you see this vehicle?

Police issued this poster to help track down suspects of the Omagh car bombing. ▶

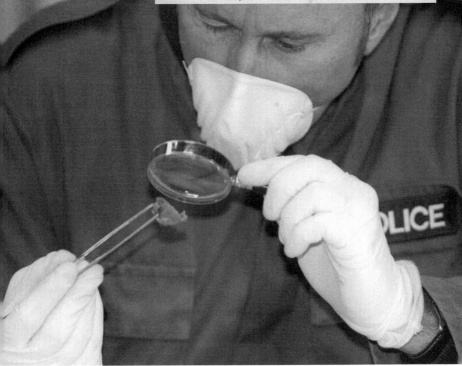

Background Police set up a wanted signboard of a suspect in the 1995 Tokyo subway nerve gas attack.

Cult of Doom

A poison-gas attack triggers fears about extremists using homemade weapons of mass death

Shoko Asahara, leader of the apocalyptic cult Aum Shinrikyo

◄ Shoko Asahara, leader of the Aum Shinrikyo cult, appeared on the cover of *Time*.

These photos identify nine of the 20 alleged Red Brigade terrorists who in 1978 kidnapped Aldo Moro and killed his five police guards.
▼

LOMBARDO Domenico
n.20.7.44
alto mt.1,70

MICALETTO Rocco
n.18/8.46
alto mt.1,68

MORETTI Mario M.
n.16.1.46
alto mt.1,68

PSCI Patrizio
n.29.7.53

PETRAMER Brunhild
n.30.8.47
alta m.1,60

ROSUCCI Susanna
n.22.5.51

GALVANI Innocente

indigente SICCA Paolo
n. 1949

Police photograph Timothy McVeigh upon his arrest in the 1995 Oklahoma City bombing case.

In 2001, Thomas Blanton, Jr., was convicted of murder in the 16th Street Baptist Church bombing in Birmingham, Alabama, in 1963. ▼

96-CR-68-M
Government Exhi

421

Date _____

95   057
04 19 95

Four judges preside over the trials of two Libyans accused in the 1988 Lockerbie bombing.

Background In Turin, Italy, Red Brigade defendants arrive in sealed police vans for another court session at the heavily fortified Lamarmora barracks.

▲
Outside court, Daniel and Susan Cohen hold a picture of their daughter Theodora, who was killed in the Lockerbie bombing.

▲
Death penalty advocates hold a candlelight vigil at dawn on the morning
Timothy McVeigh was executed.

four

Responding as
Individuals

A Victim of Terrorism Helps Others

BY SUSAN SCHINDEHETTE AND DON SIDER

Victoria Cummock lost her husband in the bombing of Pan Am Flight 103 over Lockerbie, Scotland. When she heard about the Oklahoma City bombing in 1995, she traveled there to offer whatever comfort and help she could. In the years since her husband's death, she has served on many commissions on airline safety and terrorism prevention. In an article in People, *Susan Schindehette and Don Sider describe Victoria Cummock's experiences both after her husband's death and in Oklahoma City.*

Like most Americans, Victoria Cummock was shocked by news of the Oklahoma City bombing last month. Working on paperwork at her Coral Gables, Fla., home, she heard a bulletin on the radio and recalls thinking, "Oh Lord, what have they done? Those poor, poor people and their families."

For Cummock, 42, the news from Oklahoma was, in a way, chillingly familiar. Just before Christmas of 1988, she learned that her husband, John, 38, vice president of Bacardi Foods Group and father of their three young children, was one of 270 victims of a terrorist's bomb on Pan Am Flight 103 over Lockerbie, Scotland. In the days following the crash, "I was in a fog," says Cummock, who had learned her husband was onboard only after a visit from his boss. What made her experience even more painful, she says, was that she never received an official notification of her husband's death—nor an expression of sympathy—from the White House, the State Department, or Pan Am. "I had lost my husband, my best friend, the father of my children, and my country," she says.

In the years that followed, the former model turned interior decorator would become one of the most outspoken of the Pan Am 103 family members, testifying a dozen times before Congress and playing a pivotal role in the passage of the 1990 Aviation Security Improvement Act.[1] Last month, three days after the Oklahoma bombing, which killed 168 people, Cummock phoned the White House, offering her services to the victims and even suggesting what President Clinton might say to grieving families at a planned memorial service. "Acknowledge their loss," she urged, recalling her own experiences. "Let them know in all of this that they are not alone."

On April 29, at the invitation of the Red Cross, Cummock flew to Oklahoma City to provide whatever solace she could. "I wanted to make sure the families were being looked after," she says, "and that maybe I could be a voice for them." Working out of a church near the blast site, she spent a week counseling stunned family

---

[1] Aviation Security Improvement Act—1990 law that allows the Federal Aviation Agency to fund the development of technologies capable of detecting bombs, establish the Explosives Detection Certification standard, and release FAA technology for general use.

members and rescue workers. From firsthand experience she was able to assure one young woman, who was trembling uncontrollably, that recurring nightmares of her mother, still somewhere in the ruins, would eventually stop. For a man with a missing wife, so shaken that he seemed "dazed, glazed over," says Cummock (who declines to name those she helped out of respect for their privacy), she simply offered to change the diapers of his 9-month-old baby and read a book to his $2\frac{1}{2}$-year-old daughter.

To Cummock the scene was markedly different from Lockerbie's aftermath. The Oklahoma City fire department scheduled twice-daily briefings, and family members were provided with a constant flow of information. Counselors were available, in addition to doctors and nurses. Says Cummock: "Some of [the bereaved] were getting sick to their stomachs . . . feeling like they were going to pass out. There were people there to take care of them."

Cummock urged officials not to sidestep the truth, no matter how grim. "You could see the emotions on her face, the tears, the concern," says Barbara Cienfuegos, disaster coordinator for the Los Angeles County Department of Mental Health and a Red Cross volunteer. "You could see her torment for these families." And also her toughness. "They kept calling it 'the incident,' the same way they had said, 'the Pan Am accident,'" Cummock says. "It was a bombing. Those people in Oklahoma City didn't 'pass away.' They were murdered." Telling survivors that, says Cummock, helps them to grieve—and eventually to heal.

For her efforts, Cummock has been hailed by American Red Cross president Elizabeth Dole as "a true humanitarian who has triumphed over severe personal tragedy," and one Oklahoma City survivor admiringly called her "the Mother Teresa[2] of disasters." President

---

[2] Mother Teresa—(1910–1997) in full, "Mother Teresa of Calcutta." Founder of the Missionaries of Charity, a Roman Catholic order in India that worked to help the aged and dying, as well as the blind and lepers. She was awarded the Nobel Peace Prize in 1979.

Clinton, whose April 23 memorial speech moved so many, called to thank her "for helping me find the words." Now back home in Coral Gables with her children, Christopher, 13, Matthew, 10, and Ashley, 9, Cummock downplays the praise and says of her role: "For me, it was an opportunity to give something back because I'm at a stronger place."

If so, it is only after a long and difficult recovery from her own tragedy. Cummock, whose lawsuit against Pan Am is still pending, talks to a psychotherapist four times weekly. "Not a day goes by," she says, that she doesn't think of her husband, whose ashes are buried beneath a simple granite marker in the rolling Scottish countryside, within yards of where the nose cone of Pan Am 103 fell to earth.

His most meaningful memorial, though, is something in the soul and spirit of his widow. Last month, as Cummock prepared to leave for Oklahoma City, her daughter Ashley, who had seen coverage of the blast on television, turned to her and said, "Mom, this is so sad. We're going to pray for them. But you've got to go there and tell those people they'll be all right."

QUESTIONS TO CONSIDER

1. What terrorist attack marked a personal tragedy for Victoria Cummock?

2. What sort of things did Cummock do to help the survivors of the Oklahoma City bombing?

3. Why does Cummock feel that phrases like "passed away" and "the incident" do not help people dealing with a tragedy?

4. What did the authors mean by writing that John Cummock's "most meaningful memorial . . . is something in the soul and spirit of his widow"?

Keeping Going

BY KENNY MOORE

During the 1972 Summer Olympics in Munich, West Germany, Palestinian terrorists killed two Israeli athletes and took nine others hostage. The hostages and five of their captors were all killed later in an unsuccessful rescue attempt. The Olympics are a celebration of youth, sport, and the amateur ideal—and the culmination of years of training and work for an athlete. Following the deaths, the West Germans considered canceling the rest of the Olympics; but, after a day of mourning, it was decided that the games would go on. They would continue in order to honor the dead and to deny terrorism a victory against the normal life of society. Kenny Moore was on the U.S. track and field team at those games. In a memoir, he describes how he learned of the tragedy, how he and his fellow runners prepared to go on with their races, and how it helped them to compete.

In Munich 24 years ago, Frank Shorter[1] was the only one in our fifth-floor apartment in the Athletes' Village who heard the shots. They brought him from fitful sleep

---

[1] Frank Shorter—(1947–   ) long-distance runner who, in winning the gold medal in 1972 in Munich, West Germany, became the first American in 64 years to win the marathon at the Olympic Games.

to apprehensive alertness. A few minutes later there was a pounding on the door of the coaches' room on the ground floor. U.S. track coach Bill Bowerman groggily answered it.

Before him stood Shaul Ladany, an Israeli race walker. "Can I come in?" Ladany asked, oddly, distractedly.

"What for?" growled Bowerman.

"The Arabs are in our building," said Ladany.

"Well," said Bowerman, "push them out."

"They have guns," said Ladany, who had escaped through a window when other Israelis had shouted an alarm. "Two people are dead."

Thus, as Bowerman reached to draw Ladany into the safety of his room, the coach became the first of us to know that everything had changed, that we were to be actors in the modern Olympics' great loss of innocence. At dawn we learned that after storming the building the terrorists had killed two and taken nine coaches and athletes hostage. From the balcony of our apartment, which Shorter and I shared with fellow U.S. runners Jon Anderson, Mike Manley, Steve Savage and Dave Wottle, we could see tanks, troops, and emergency vehicles assembling 150 yards away, behind the blocky building that housed the Israelis, among others. We took turns on our terrace all day, nervously plucking seeds from a fennel plant that grew there and grinding them into our palms, keeping vigil.

Shorter agonized quietly. "Imagine how it must be for them in there," he said as the singsong European police sirens sounded. "Some maniac with a machine gun saying, 'Let's kill 'em now,' and another one saying, 'No, let's wait awhile.' How long could you stand that?"

In mid-afternoon, after competition had continued as scheduled, word came: The Games had been stopped. The IOC[2] would not say when, or even whether, they

---

[2] IOC—International Olympic Committee.

would resume. In that uncertainty, we experienced level after level of grief. I remember weeping for my own event, the marathon, for years of preparation that seemed wasted, and for the violated sanctuary of the Games. It truly did not hit me until then, in my 29th year, that the Olympics were not somehow immune to every threat to which the larger world was subject.

I was not alone. Steve Prefontaine, the 5,000-meter runner, raged at the terrorists' blindness, at what, to him, was their sheer, malignant nerve. "These are our Games," he cried. "Anyone who would murder us for some demented cause just proves himself incapable of understanding what we do."

The terrorists were demanding a helicopter to carry them and their hostages to a plane that would take them out of the country. Negotiations went on into darkness. At 10, I tried to escape the Village and discovered shouting crowds of athletes and officials being turned back from the gates. We were sealed in.

Through rising **furor**,[3] I went back to the apartment. From the balcony we watched a flight of helicopters suddenly drop down and land near where the standoff was. The **cacophony**[4] of their engines echoing off the concrete buildings was such that we, spooked, thought it was machine-gun fire.

Within the hour the helicopters lifted off again, on their way to Furstenfeldbruck Air Base, where a plane was waiting, and much else. They disappeared into a cloudy sky that I remember as roiled and reddened by searchlights. Shorter watched the sky long after the rest of us had finished our prayers for the Israelis' safe passage. "You know, Kenny," he said with shaken softness, "I don't think it's over."

---

[3] **furor**—noisy disturbance; uproar.

[4] **cacophony**—harsh, unpleasant sound.

In the morning we learned the final horror. The Germans had misjudged the number of terrorists. There had been too few police marksmen waiting at Furstenfeldbruck. When they opened fire, one unhurt terrorist set off a grenade.

I awakened to see Anderson holding a German newspaper with photos of a burned-out helicopter. Prefontaine translated the headline for me: SIXTEEN DEAD. That was when he said, "They could load us all on a plane right now to take us home, and I'd go." He heard no dissent.

There was a memorial service for our fellow Olympians in the main stadium, where IOC president Avery Brundage announced that the Games would go on, after a 24-hour postponement. Our response to that, individually and severally, defines us still.

Shorter and I were in the marathon. We knew it was impossible to protect us on the route. We knew also that the British team had received death threats from the IRA, a case of a second set of terrorists piggybacking on the first. Yet there was never any question that we would run. "We have to not let this detract from our performance," said Shorter, "because that's what they want."

I can't speak for Frank, but I know I ran the 1972 Olympic marathon expressly measuring my own suffering against that of my fellow Olympians. Every time I would get a stitch in my side, or a cramp running up a hamstring, I would ask myself if this passing ache were comparable to what they felt in that phosphorous **conflagration**.[5] That settled, I would run on, chastened.

Shorter won. I was fourth. We ran well, and in that we were emblematic of the essential lesson of all athletics: Everyone suffers. It's what you do with your suffering that lifts and advances us, as swimmers, softball players and gymnasts. As a species.

---

[5] **conflagration**—large fire.

When former Atlanta mayor Andrew Young was asked to respond to the Centennial Park bombing,[6] he pointed out that the rest of the world has been enduring such events for years, and then quoted Martin Luther King, Jr., who said, "Violence is the language of the unheard." Yes, but it's a language of obscenity. The terrorists of 1972 were fanatics, prepared, perhaps even content, to die for their cause. They were in some ways the mirror image of Olympians, except from their suffering they brought forth death. They had surrendered to the eternal cycle of violence in which the sins of the fathers are visited upon their sons. They were every victim become destroyer.

We were fortunate enough to know better. We were successors to the great moral advance made by the Greeks in 776 B.C. when they came to understand that there is more honor in outrunning a man than in killing him, when they so sanctified the Games that they would lay down their arms during the sacred truce of Olympia and grant participants free passage through warring states. Our answer to the attack in 1972 was 2,748 years old: performance, transforming performance.

When he heard the news of the Atlanta bombing, Shorter called me. "On that balcony in Munich," he said, "it was like, someone is doing this to them over there. But in Atlanta, now, it is a different kind of fear. The bomb was set in the public precincts. The feeling is that we're all the target now."

Yet the IOC, ACOG[7] and the White House never seriously considered stopping the Atlanta Games. "It was a slow process in Munich," said Shorter. "The day

---

[6] Centennial Park bombing—On July 27, 1996, a crude homemade bomb exploded at the Centennial Olympic Games in Atlanta in a park where there were thousands of people. The blast resulted in two deaths and many injuries.

[7] ACOG—Atlanta Committee for the Olympic Games, an organization responsible for running the 1996 Summer Olympic Games.

we watched as the hostages were held and the day off for the memorial service, we went through the stages humans must go through in times of brutal stress: from denial to anger, to grief, to resolve. It's like Atlanta learned from that. This time officials went straight to affirming that the Games will go on."

As did the athletes. "It's difficult to focus on goals when someone is trying to destroy the Olympic spirit," said Gail Devers, after winning the women's 100 in an almost defiant fashion. "That's what they're trying to do, and I'm not going to let them."

I could hear echoes of '72 in the reaction of U.S. judoka Jimmy Pedro, a bronze medalist in the 157-pound division: "I worked 19 years to be here. The athletes won't leave, we won't stop. Of course we'll go on."

The striking thing was his tone, so offhand, so expectant that everyone in the world will understand that his—ours—is a perfectly obvious course, to turn pain into performance. But of course they don't all understand, or we wouldn't have our latest dead, or children torn and broken by explosives detonated, incomprehensibly, to make some point. What Shorter said on that Munich balcony was and remains true. It's not over, not until all the cycles of violence are broken and man is perfected, which isn't going to be any Olympiad soon.

So the Olympian thing to do is simply to spread the word that barbarism only makes Olympians stronger. "We've got to talk about the risks," says Shorter. "Know the percentages, so people can't deny the risks, but then we have to go forward, because to surrender here is to surrender all. We have to say to ourselves, as a society, what we said before that marathon back in Munich. We have to say, 'This is as scared as I get. Now let's go run.'"

QUESTIONS TO CONSIDER

1. Why do you think the writer believed that before the events of 1972 the Olympic Games might be "immune to every threat" from the outside world?

2. Why did the 1972 attack make the American runner Steve Prefontaine so angry?

3. If you had been an athlete at the Munich games, would you have wanted them to continue after the terrorist incident? How do you think the deaths of fellow athletes might have affected your performance?

4. Why does the writer feel that terrorists are in some ways the "mirror image" of Olympic athletes?

5. How do the attitudes of these athletes show the "right response" to terrorism?

What Is "Normal"?

The immediate reaction to a terrorist attack is to want vengeance, to want the government and military to strike back at the terrorists. It is a natural reaction to violence and pain. Everyone wants to do something, but in such a situation the only thing to do is to go on with life as usual. The violence and destruction of the September 11 attacks were obvious locally, but it also greatly disrupted life around the country. Many parts of the economy, such as the airline industry, were hard hit. Tourism dropped to such a point that the mayor of New York, when asked what people could do for the city, suggested they "go to a play." It is hard at first to go back to the usual worries and activities, but the daily needs reassert themselves. In two short essays, Nancy Gibbs in Time *magazine and novelist Jonathan Franzen in* The New Yorker *describe their reactions to the September 11 attacks and then consider how we are different and how we must go on.*

What Comes Next?
by Nancy Gibbs

What happens when you are told to go back to your normal life but have trouble finding your way there?

This is what the U.S. government asks of its citizens. "Enjoy life," President Bush says. "Go down to Disney World." Because it is normal to want to have fun. Buy stocks, say the Wall Street cheerleaders, boost the market, because it is normal to want to get rich. Feel your feelings, say the grief counselors, because anger is normal and anguish is cleansing and there's nowhere to hide in any case. A party store in Texas gets an order for 10 of its Osama bin Laden piñatas from a California therapist who says she wants them for her patients. Take a gamble, come to Las Vegas, say the ads for the convention bureau, because "it's time to get away." But that doesn't mean we are arriving at normal.

Or that we ever will again, if normal means Sept. 10. In our mourning for the way we were, there is some comfort in admitting that our world back then was not as safe as we thought; and it may not now be quite as dangerous as it seems. It helps to find people whose fears are whirling out of control, because they make you feel sane and brave by comparison. A rich couple in Coral Gables, Fla., buys gas masks and chemical suits for the whole family; bemused neighbors inquire whether they are designer label. At least one Hollywood celebrity asks his security consultant about liquidating assets[1] and burying gold in his backyard. OUTBREAK TRAINING reads the sign on the door of the Iowa Public Health Department. Smallpox? Or chicken pox?

What officials did in public, the public did in miniature. We are all intelligence officers now. Two hundred people showed up for "Middle East 101" at Christ Community Church in Idaho Falls, Idaho. Books on biological warfare,[2] the Taliban and terrorism are selling out; so is the Koran,[3] and maps of Afghanistan. "Is there an *Islam for Dummies*?" asks a guest at a dinner party in

---

[1] liquidating assets—turning stocks, real estate and other valuables into cash by selling them.

[2] biological warfare—use of infectious microscopic organisms dispersed as airborne clouds to kill or seriously injure people over a very large area. Development and use of biological weapons has been repeatedly outlawed by international agreements, and such weapons have never been used in battle.

[3] Koran—also spelled Quran, the holy book of Islam.

Des Moines, Iowa. We're spending a lot on defense right now, enlisting sentries and maintaining checkpoints that provide the kind of security we need to go about our business. Smell the tap water before you drink it. Carry extra cash. Plan your escape route.

"It's very hard to fight a guerrilla war with conventional forces," President Bush said, which is why the action was elsewhere last week. The armies were indeed at war, but for the moment it was the armies of foreign ministers and finance wizards and spooks and geeks and anyone who could somehow trap and strangle the enemy. Meanwhile, the new generals of Homeland Security tried to button down the country, knowing that any U.S. attack is likely to trigger a retaliatory strike and that this time we need to be ready. We will just have to get used to something we have never seen: the regular sight of soldiers on our streets, in the airports, at the malls. In Los Angeles security guards were searching old ladies' pocketbooks as they arrived at the Tony Bennett concert. There are no more public tours of the Alabama Army depot where they store 2,254 tons of nerve gas[4] shells. There are no White House tours either.

Time asked people whether life had returned to normal since the attacks; 60% of Americans said it had. But normal is a homier place than before, full of chocolate and creamy food, maybe some bottled water in the basement. Children's librarians say that parents are asking for old friends such as *Goodnight Moon* and *The Borrowers*, looking for a soft path to guide their children toward sleep. You can finally walk into the Radio Shack in Oconomowoc, Wis., without finding people glued to the seven TVs. Patriotism is normal, not sentimental or defiant or retro. At an Iowa orthodontist's office, kids are choosing red-white-and-blue braces. "It's because of

---

[4] nerve gas—gaseous form of chemical agents such as Sarin, VX, and soman whose effects are similar to insecticides: respiratory problems, vomiting, loss of vision, paralysis, and finally death.

all the things that are happening," explains Katie Slocum, 12, flashing a sweet, self-conscious smile of patriotic metal.

Normal is a line that rocks and weaves; you have to chase it. In New York it means leaving home two hours earlier if you have to drive over a bridge, because it takes a while for the guards to crawl over and under and through every 18-wheeler that is trying to get into Manhattan. But it was a comfort in the midtown crush, finally, to hear a driver yell, "Hey, move the car, jerk!" and sense the return of vehicular hostility; that felt like normal too. Miss America visited ground zero, as did Paul Newman and John Travolta and the cast of *The Sopranos*. The war zone is a shrine, and a circus. The funerals are coming faster now, 16 on Saturday alone; the mayor tried to send an official to each one. Elsewhere, friends get together for dinner and play a game: Let's See How Long We Can Go Without Talking About It. The answer so far: not very long. But it may just take more practice.

If you are trying to find your way back, it doesn't help to have to pass armed guards with grenades strapped to their chests at Boston's Logan Airport, or to hear that there are generals authorized to shoot a passenger jet out of the sky should they conclude that it poses a threat. The metal detectors are so sensitive that an underwire bra will trip them. So will a candy wrapper. Yet a federal marshal was able to slip through with a buck knife in his pocket. Thus many passengers, returning to the skies last week, resorted to their own incantations: It's never been safer to fly. Lightning doesn't strike twice. If I stay home, they win.

Tragedy has frisked us all. We are finding out what we are carrying around that no one knew we had. Maybe normal is not a useful word for now, too slippery and glib. Maybe transcendence for the moment lies with routine, doing the same things as before, even if we do them differently, with a heavier heart or a lighter touch or a glance over our shoulder. The rescue workers keep saying that they are just doing their jobs. And so they invite us to do the same.

What Do We Do?
by Jonathan Franzen

The one recurring nightmare I've had for many years is about the end of the world, and it goes like this. In a crowded, modern cityscape not unlike lower Manhattan, I'm flying a jetliner down an avenue where everything is wrong. It seems impossible that the buildings to either side of me won't shear my wings off, impossible that I can keep the plane aloft while moving at such a low speed. The way is always blocked, but somehow I manage to turn a sharp corner or to pilot the plane beneath an overpass, only to confront a skyscraper so high that I would have to rise vertically to clear it. As I pull the plane into a dismayingly shallow climb, the skyscraper looms and rushes forward to meet me, and I wake up, with unspeakable relief, in my ordinary bed.

Last Tuesday there was no awakening. You found your way to a TV and watched. Unless you were a very good person indeed, you were probably, like me, experiencing the collision of several incompatible worlds inside your head. Besides the horror and sadness of what you were watching, you might also have felt a childish disappointment over the disruption of your day, or a selfish worry about the impact on your finances, or admiration for an attack so brilliantly conceived and so flawlessly executed, or, worst of all, an awed appreciation of the visual spectacle it produced.

Never mind whether certain Palestinians were or were not dancing in the streets. Somewhere—you can be absolutely sure of this—the death artists who planned the attack were rejoicing over the terrible beauty of the towers' collapse. After years of dreaming and working and hoping, they were now experiencing a fulfillment as overwhelming as any they could have allowed themselves to pray for. Perhaps some of these glad artists were hiding in ruined Afghanistan, where the average life expectancy is barely forty. In that world you can't walk through a bazaar without seeing men and children who are missing limbs.

In *this* world, where the Manhattan skyline has now been maimed and the scorched wreckage at the Pentagon is reminiscent of Kabul,[5] I'm trying to imagine what I don't want to imagine: the scene inside a plane one moment before impact. At the controls, a terrorist is raising a prayer of thanks to Allah in expectation of instant transport from this world to the next one, where houris[6] will presently reward him for his glorious success. At the back of the cabin, huddled Americans are trembling and moaning and, no doubt, in many cases, praying to their God for a diametrically opposite outcome. And then, a moment later, for hijacker and hijacked alike, the world ends.

On the street, after the impact, survivors spoke of being delivered from death by God's guidance and grace. But even they, the survivors, were stumbling out of the smoke into a different world. Who would have guessed that everything could end so suddenly on a pretty Tuesday morning? In the space of two hours, we left behind a happy era of Game Boy economics and trophy houses and entered a world of fear and vengeance. Even if you'd been waiting for the nineties-ending crash[7] throughout the nineties, even if you'd believed all along that further terrorism in New York was only a matter of when and not of whether, what you felt on Tuesday morning wasn't intellectual satisfaction, or simply empathetic horror, but deep grief for the loss of daily life in prosperous, forgetful times: the traffic

---

[5] Kabul—Afghanistan's largest city and capital.

[6] houris—beautiful women who inhabit the Islamic paradise.

[7] nineties-ending crash—anticipated end to the American economic boom of the later 1990s.

jammed by delivery trucks and unavailable cabs, "Apocalypse Now Redux" in local theatres, your date for drinks downtown on Wednesday, the sixty-three homers of Barry Bonds, the hourly AOL[8] updates on J. Lo's doings. On Monday morning, the front-page headline in the *News* had been "KIPS BAY TENANTS SAY: WE'VE GOT KILLER MOLD." This front page is (and will, for a while, remain) amazing.

The challenge in the old world, the nineties world of Bill Clinton, was to remember that, behind the prosperity and complacency, death was waiting and entire countries hated us. The problem of the new world, the zeroes world of George Bush, will be to reassert the ordinary, the trivial, and even the ridiculous in the face of instability and dread: to mourn the dead and then try to awaken to our small humanities and our pleasurable daily nothing-much.

---

[8] AOL—short for America Online, company started in 1991 that had become the world's largest Internet service provider by 1999.

QUESTIONS TO CONSIDER

1. According to Nancy Gibbs, how did average Americans react to the terrorist attacks? In your opinion, how are some responses better or healthier than others?

2. How do you think the process of getting back to normal might be helped by "admitting that our world back then [before the attacks] was not as safe as we thought"?

3. How can "normal" mean different things to different people? What is your opinion of using the word *normal* in discussing people's responses to terrorism?

4. What are some of the features of the "new world" that Jonathan Franzen feels began on September 11, 2001?

5. What do you think Franzen means by "our pleasurable daily nothing-much"?

Should We Be Afraid?

BY LARRY LAUDAN

*Terrorists' goal is to make people afraid, and the tremendous
media coverage of their attacks is generally successful in making
people fear air travel, government buildings, working in skyscrapers,
riding the subway, and so on. Our chances, however, of being hurt
in a terrorist attack are very small compared to our chances of
being in a car accident or falling while stepping out of the shower.
Logic tells us not to fear the terrorists' weapons, but it is hard to
overcome the fears inspired by the violence. In an article from
1996, Professor Larry Laudan asks whether we are being logical
when we fear terrorism and pour billions of dollars into fighting it.*

Those who make their living studying risks are con-
tinually surprised and sometimes appalled by the
willingness of the public to fixate their fears on threats
which are—objectively considered—relatively minor,
while ignoring those things which pose more sizable
risks. For the past year or so, we have been in the midst

of a media frenzy about domestic terrorism. Triggered by the blast in Oklahoma City,[1] fueled by the recent crash of TWA Flight 800[2] and the pipe bomb in Atlanta,[3] the media have created an atmosphere of fear and trembling among the citizenry about terrorism.

Witness the fact that President Clinton and congressional leaders have joined hands in a photogenic and bipartisan fight against terrorism, designed chiefly to calm the nerves of jittery Americans. Witness, too, the number of people who stay clear of federal buildings these days or who at least consider whether to cancel their next flight. Everyone is beginning to ask: "Am I the next victim?"

Certain responses are right on target in the face of such acts of terrorism—principally moral outrage at the cowardly perpetrators and compassion for the victims and their families. But fear for oneself and one's life should not be in the cards since the risk that the average American will be a victim of terrorism is extremely remote.

Contrary to media hype, domestic terrorism is not a creation of the mid-1990s. During the 1980s, for instance, the United States had a score of political assassinations, more than 100 politically motivated bombings, almost 50 hijackings of aircraft and a handful of episodes of sabotage and hostage-taking by those with a political axe to grind. Even so, the numbers do not amount to much of a threat. In fact, your annual risk of being killed in a terrorist incident in the United States is about one in half a million.

---

[1] Oklahoma City—site of the worst incident of domestic terrorism in U.S. history, the bombing of a federal building in 1995 that left 168 people dead.

[2] TWA Flight 800—transatlantic flight that mysteriously blew up off the coast of Long Island, New York, in July 1996; the disaster was officially declared by investigators *not* to be the work of terrorists.

[3] pipe bomb in Atlanta—crude explosive device contained in a metal pipe; one went off at the Olympic Games in Atlanta in 1996.

An event like the TWA 800 disaster would have to recur every two or three days before your risk of being a terrorist victim even approached your risk of being an ordinary murder victim. You are 40 times more likely to be killed by a drunk driver than to be wiped out by a terrorist's bomb. More of us are killed by falling objects than by terrorist activity. The point is that—in that long catalogue of nasty things that may happen to you—terrorism comes much closer to the bottom of the list than it does to the top.

What does it matter if people get exercised[4] about a risk that is in fact quite remote? Principally, it matters because such concern has a way of translating itself both into dollars spent and into liberties curtailed. We are already seeing **palpable**[5] signs of both here, with the feds aiming to invest billions more in anti-terrorism efforts and with numerous proposals floating through Congress further to restrict our civil liberties in the name of stamping out terrorism. Both are misguided. Those billions could go more effectively into reducing much more common and costly risks, such as drunk drivers on the highways or ordinary, run-of-the-mill homicides. Where our freedom is concerned, are we really prepared to arrive two hours early for every domestic flight and be subject to body searches because our appearance might fit some security guard's profile of a potential trouble-maker?

The politicians keep telling us that we mustn't let the terrorists win by forcing us to change our habits or our way of life. But this gutsy business-as-usual line is belied[6] by the same officials telling us that we should spend extra billions on security and that all of us should take added precautions, given this danger in our midst. No one at the senior levels of government or in the

---

[4] exercised—become upset.

[5] **palpable**—obvious.

[6] belied—contradicted.

media is saying what is both true and would be the most effective weapon against the terrorist, namely, that the risk posed by domestic terrorism does not amount to a hill of beans and that we are not going to permit it to alter how we perceive the world or conduct ourselves.

QUESTIONS TO CONSIDER

1. What is Larry Laudan's main argument about the connection between fear and terrorism?

2. What responses to terrorism does Laudan say are "right on target"?

3. Why does Laudan worry about people being afraid of a threat "that is in fact quite remote"?

4. What do you feel about Laudan's view that government anti-terrorism efforts are "misguided"?

5. In your opinion, why is it helpful or not helpful to remember the low odds of being killed or injured in a terrorist attack?

Helping Children Understand

INTERVIEW WITH HAROLD KOPLEWICZ

Explaining terrorism is difficult for the experts. Helping children to understand attacks like Oklahoma City or the World Trade Center is even more so. In a speech, President Bush described a little girl who, when told that terrorists wouldn't hate Americans if they knew who they were, asked, "Can't we just tell them all our names?" How do you present faceless evil and complex political and religious movements to children? How can you explain the deaths of 5,000 people? In an article from People, *child psychiatrist Harold Koplewicz discusses how children handle such crises and what parents can do.*

Accustomed to dealing with the anxieties of others, psychiatrist Harold Koplewicz recently faced his own deepest fears. Koplewicz, 48, director of the New York University Child Study Center, was watching TV while exercising in the gym of his Upper East Side building on the morning of Sept. 11 when he saw footage of the first plane hitting the World Trade Center. "My gut response was, 'Are my children safe?'" says Koplewicz, who immediately left to find the two youngest of his three sons, Adam, 15, and Sam, 13, at their schools and bring them home. They were joined later by his wife, Linda Sirow, 48, a teacher at Manhattan's Dalton School.

Once reassured that his family was out of harm's way, Koplewicz, who specializes in treating children, turned his attention to the needs of the 1.1 million students in New York City's public schools. At the request of Chancellor Harold Levy, Koplewicz's staff worked through the night to prepare materials for teachers on how to help the children in the aftermath of the attack. These suggestions are built on experience. Koplewicz treated a group of New York City elementary school students who had been on a field trip to the W T C in 1993 when a terrorist bomb exploded. "Frequently kids don't express their feelings," he says. "It's important that parents be able to recognize symptoms and know how to help them." Koplewicz spoke with correspondent Fannie Weinstein about what parents can do to help their children cope.

Is there a "normal" reaction kids might have to what happened?

Normal can be anywhere from no symptoms to having difficulty sleeping and concentrating, and asking the same questions over and over. The warning sign of trouble is a change in your child's personality. For instance, if you have a **gregarious**[1] kid who suddenly seems much more somber. The first line of attack should be reassurance, and then a discussion about what happened in words they can understand. There's no need to jump in with professional help if they seem different for a few weeks. But if these behaviors persist, it's time to intervene.

How about adults?

If someone doesn't want to go out or has trouble falling asleep or is even weeping for days, that's okay.

---

[1] **gregarious**—sociable, outgoing.

But if someone who didn't lose anybody says to you, "I'm filled with grief," and they're sobbing and they just don't seem to snap out of it, then it's time to go for some help.

Is the child's age a factor?

Definitely. Nursery school-age kids are going to be focused on personal safety; the way they show that is they start to regress. They may not want to sleep in their bed alone. They may become angry and frustrated. This calls for a lot of comforting. Tell your child that he or she is safe, that Mommy and Daddy are safe, that their school is safe. It also helps to get back into routines.

Grade schoolers may become less independent and more clinging. These children too need a lot of reassurance. They're also likely to have obsessive thoughts about the attack. They may want to talk about what happened again and again. It's okay to answer their questions, but you don't want to give them too much information because it will likely make them more anxious.

And teens?

Adolescents exhibit more symptoms because they have much more angst[2] to begin with. They're likely to be more irritable, more sullen. They're also likely to be very angry, and because they already have a certain bravado about them, they may say things like, "Let's level Afghanistan." The way they control their anxiety is aggression. That's why with them, your discussions have to include the notion of tolerance.

Should kids be allowed to watch TV coverage of the attack and its aftermath?

Children under 5 shouldn't watch any programs on which they're going to talk about the attack. I wouldn't let kids between 6 and 12 watch the news by themselves, and I would limit them to a half hour or an hour a day of this coverage. With adolescents, we can't control what

---

[2] angst—fearfulness, often accompanied by depression.

they see, but we can make every attempt to discuss it with them. You have to be the voice of reason for them.

Can taking part in relief efforts help children and adults feel better?

Yes. One way to help a child regain control of his or her feelings is to have them do something active. For instance, you can suggest having a bake sale. With teens, you might suggest donating blood. For adults too, now is a good time to help people who are less fortunate.

Should children attend funerals and memorial services?

Our religious rituals are wonderful in that they help us move along. But seeing people completely lose it is very unsettling for kids. For you to show them you are upset is perfectly appropriate—if you're not hysterical.

Is it okay to want to move on?

Psychologically, we have to move on because we know that continuous hopelessness puts us at more risk of depression. But there's no doubt we're going to be more fearful. I walked by the Empire State Building the other day, and I felt my heart race a little faster. But then I thought to myself, "I'm not going to allow myself to be terrorized by what happened." That's what we have to say to ourselves, and our actions, in turn, will say that to our children.

QUESTIONS TO CONSIDER

1. According to the psychiatrist Harold Koplewicz, how is a child's age a factor in how he or she reacts to a terrorist attack?

2. What are normal reactions to terrorist-induced tragedy on the part of children? How do they differ from those of adults?

3. How would you help young children you know deal with the aftermath of a terrorist incident?

What's the Best Memorial to the Victims?

Memorials take many forms, but all the finest have in common that they are sites of emotional release. The shell of a surviving building in Hiroshima is a powerful reminder of the terrible destruction wrought by the first atomic bomb. Different but equally powerful is the Vietnam Veterans Memorial in Washington, D.C., where the inclusion of the name of each dead American soldier has an overwhelming effect on their surviving friends and relations. In other cases the memorial is less physical. The finest memorial to the Holocaust is the state of Israel, and the real memorial to the Japanese-Americans interned during World War II is a stronger national commitment to diversity and tolerance and law. The question of how to memorialize the victims of September 11 arose within days of the attacks. Some said that the World Trade Center site should be left as it is to remind all of what happened. Others thought the towers ought to be rebuilt to establish the power of our values and memorialize the victims by carrying on with their work. It will take time and much controversy to decide on a memorial. An October 2001 article from The New York Times *by*

Hans Butzer, the architect who designed the memorial for the victims of the 1995 Oklahoma City bombing, is followed by two letters to the editor of the newspaper.

Deciding What Our Loss Means
by Hans Butzer

Although it is natural to want to envision how America ought to memorialize those who died in the Sept. 11 terrorist attacks, it is still too soon to begin to design any kind of memorial for the dead.

We need to address some fundamental questions about the event itself before we can turn to questions of how to mark what happened. For example, was this one tragedy or four? Will there be one memorial or four—in Virginia, Pennsylvania, and (two?) in New York? If there is more than one, will the efforts to create them be coordinated? Perhaps most important: Who is the "we" that will make these and other difficult decisions?

What has proved so important to the community of Oklahoma City since the bombing of the Alfred P. Murrah Federal Building[1] in April 1995 is that these decisions were made primarily in a forum open to a variety of viewpoints. Shortly after the attack a committee was established, through the governor's office, of 350 people in the community—politicians, business people, members of victims' families, survivors, rescuers and others whose lives had been changed. The meetings of this committee were considered by many who took part in them to be the memorials themselves.

Just as some have proposed that the World Trade Center towers rise again, some proposed that the Murrah building be rebuilt, suggesting that this would be both a memorial and a statement of defiance. But as the discussions continued, opinions became less

---

[1] Alfred P. Murrah Federal Building—Oklahoma City building destroyed by a terrorist bomb blast in 1995 that left 168 people dead.

absolute. With time, the community came to realize that what was most important was to focus on the lives that had been lost or changed forever. The committee crafted a mission statement, which established the goals for the memorial, laying out some specific requests (for example that the memorial include no statues or photographs of people).

A year and a half passed between the April bombing and the announcement of an international design competition. While the vision for the memorial was presented in the form of the mission statement, its actual design was selected through a two-stage competition by a jury made up of designers and local people. The design by my company may have best fulfilled the mission statement because it was conceived as a story; the key to experiencing it is having to move through the formal entry gates that act as bookends. To the south is a field of 168 empty chairs for the victims; to the north is a lone American elm that survived the bombing.

For those who now struggle to understand the attacks of Sept. 11, the task may seem even more daunting. The scale of the physical impact and loss of life seems, if possible, further beyond comprehension than that in Oklahoma City. Undoubtedly, property owners will discover that plowing under the site to rebuild may prove more difficult than first imagined. But more important is not to try to describe the design of the memorial too specifically too soon. First, politicians, property owners and community leaders should develop a forum to allow those who see themselves as shareholders to participate in a meaningful way. Working together to achieve a consensus will be just as much a memorial as any construct that is built.

Letters to the Editor

The best memorial for the victims of the World Trade Center terrorism would not be architectural. Our true monument to the Triangle Shirtwaist Factory fire[2] of 1911 is in our labor laws. Our true monument to the victims of the Ku Klux Klan[3] is in our civil rights laws and the growing black middle class. Our true monument to the Pearl Harbor attack is not in Hawaii but in modern Japan.

Yes, we should have a physical memorial to the dead, but the true memorial in a vibrant society would be the elimination of the fundamentalist threat.

SETH STEINBERG
New York, Oct. 10, 2001

Regarding a memorial for the World Trade Center victims, let's include more sacred outdoor places. It is not in the American character, except in the Native American belief system, to think in terms of sacred outdoor places.

When most of us think of sacred places, we think of monuments and buildings like churches, synagogues, mosques and temples, but sacred places are also open to the elements and outdoors.

A few sacred places in downtown New York City, like Trinity Church and St. Paul Chapel, survived, and we residents of Lower Manhattan say that's miraculous. But where are our sacred groves? Creating sacred places was once part of the American character.

PEARL DUNCAN
New York, Oct. 10, 2001

---

[2] Triangle Shirtwaist Factory fire—clothing factory fire in New York City in which nearly 150 women workers died. It called attention to the need for improved working conditions in the garment industry.

[3] Ku Klux Klan—secret organization violently opposed to African Americans, Jews, Catholics, and foreigners. The Klan used terrorist methods against those it viewed as enemies.

QUESTIONS TO CONSIDER

1. What is the process Hans Butzer describes the Oklahoma City community as having followed to create a memorial to the 1995 bombing?

2. Why do you think the process followed in creating a memorial might be as important to a community as the actual monument that is built?

3. What does Seth Steinberg mean when he writes that our "true monument to the victims of the Ku Klux Klan is in our civil rights laws"?

4. How do you feel about the three viewpoints in this selection?

5. Why do you think creating memorials is an important way of allowing individuals to respond to terrorism?

All the national flags at the 1972 Munich Olympics are flown at half-staff in memory of the 11 Israeli athletes killed by Arab terrorists. ▶

Preserving Memories

▲

Hundreds march down the street as part of the funeral parade for the victims of the 1998 car bombing in Omagh, Northern Ireland.

Pope John Paul II visits the tomb of former Italian prime minister Aldo Moro, who was kidnapped and murdered by Red Brigade terrorists in 1978.

Civil rights leaders including Martin Luther King, Jr., (third from right) are in Birmingham at the memorial service for the four girls killed in the 16th Street Baptist Church bombing in 1963.

▼

Kenneth Hawkes visits the grave of his fiancée, Esther Gibson, who was killed in the Omagh car bombing.

World leaders attend Rajiv Gandhi's funeral in 1991. ▼

Background Sonia Gandhi sits in mourning after the assassination of her husband, Rajiv Gandhi.

In
Remembrance
of
all victims of
Lockerbie Air Disaster
who died on
21st December 1988

N DAVID AKERSTROM
LE ELISE BOULANGE!
HAEL WARREN BUS
VALERIE CANADY

▲

Names of the victims are etched in stone at the Pan Am flight 103 memorial in Lockerbie, Scotland.

◄ Bert Ammerman visits the memorial stone at Lockerbie to remember his brother Thomas, a victim aboard the doomed airliner.

▲
Jimmy Boldien hugs the chair of his aunt Laura Jane Garrison in the Field of Empty Chairs at the Oklahoma City National Memorial.

◀ At the Oklahoma City National Memorial, the moment after the bombing is forever carved into the monument called the Gates of Time.

Chronology of Terrorism Since World War II

1945—World War II ends.

1948—Jewish terrorists kill hundreds of Arabs in the Palestinian village of Deir Yassin. The State of Israel is founded in Palestine as a Jewish homeland.

1954—Algerian nationalists begin terrorist campaign against French colonial rule.

1960—Police kill 69 anti-apartheid protestors at Sharpeville, in northeastern South Africa. Sharpeville massacre prompts increased use of terrorism by anti-apartheid groups in South Africa.

1963—Civil rights demonstrations in Birmingham, Alabama, prompt terrorist attacks by white racists. 16th Street Baptist Church is bombed, killing four African-American girls.

1964—Palestine Liberation Organization (PLO) founded.

1967—Israel occupies territories of West Bank and Gaza Strip after winning the Six Day War.

1968—Popular Front for the Liberation of Palestine (PFLP) hijacks an El Al flight from Rome on July 22 and diverts it to Algeria. Terrorists hold Israelis aboard hostage until August 31.

1969—Non-violent Catholic civil rights protests in Northern Ireland spark a long period of violence between Catholics and Protestants, which continues into the 1990s; militant groups on both sides engage in terrorism.

1972—Irish Republican Army (IRA) "Bloody Friday" bombing attacks in Belfast, Northern Ireland, kill 9 people. PFLP and Japanese Red Army terrorists kill 28 people at Israel's Lod Airport. 11 Israeli athletes are killed when they are taken hostage by Arab terrorists at the Olympic Games in Munich, West Germany.

1973—U.S. angers Arabs by supporting Israel against Egypt and Syria in the Yom Kippur War.

1976—Terrorists of the Baader-Meinhof Gang and the Popular Front for the liberation of Palestine hijack an Air France plane and force it to fly to Entebbe airport in Uganda; Israeli commandos later free 103 hostages in the first major counterattack against hijackings.

1977—Terrorists of the Baader-Meinhof Gang kidnap German industrialist Hanns-Martin Schleyer in Cologne, West Germany; he is later killed.

1978—Red Brigade terrorists kidnap former Italian premier Aldo Moro on March 16; his body is found on May 9. Theodore J. Kaczynski, known as the Unabomber, begins his serial bombing campaign; over the next 17 years, 3 people are killed and 23 injured in the 16 bombings attributed to him. Camp David Accords signed by Israel's Menachem Begin and Egypt's Anwar Sadat.

1979—On November 4, radical Iranian students seize 52 American hostages at the U.S. embassy in Tehran. They are held for 444 days.

1979–1989—Afghan War fought between invading Soviet troops and Afghan mujahideen guerrillas.

1981—Anwar Sadat is assassinated by the radical Al Jihad movement. Hundreds of villagers in El Mozote, El Salvador, are killed by government troops.

1983—Suicide truck bomb attack kills 63 people at the U.S. Embassy in Beirut, Lebanon. Another truck bomb destroys the Marine barracks in Beirut, killing 241 Americans. Both attacks are the work of Islamic Jihad, a Muslim fundamentalist group.

1984—Sikh terrorists seized the Golden Temple in Amritsar, India; hundreds die after the shrine is retaken by Indian security forces. Indira Gandhi, prime minister of India, is later killed by her Sikh bodyguards.

1985—PLO terrorists seize an Italian cruise liner, the *Achille Lauro*, in the eastern Mediterranean; a passenger, Leon Klinghoffer, is killed.

1986—Bombing of a night club in Berlin, by a Palestinian with the help of Libyan agents, kills two people, one a U.S. soldier. Ten days later, U.S. bombs Libya in reprisal.

1987—Palestinians begin a rebellion, the *intifada* (Arabic, "uprising"), against Israeli occupation; it continues until 1993. Terry Waite is kidnapped by Hezbollah terrorists in January; Waite is held prisoner for nearly 5 years.

1988—Pan Am Flight 103 is destroyed by a bomb over Lockerbie, Scotland, killing all 259 people aboard and 11 people on the ground.

1991—U.S. fights Persian Gulf War against Iraq. Former Indian prime minister Rajiv Gandhi is killed by Tamil Tiger suicide bomber in Sriperumbudur, India.

1992—Three bombings target U.S. soldiers in Yemen; these are the first attacks by Osama bin Laden's terrorist organization al-Qaeda.

1993—A truck bomb exploded by radical Muslims in a parking garage under the World Trade Center kills six people.

1994—Jewish right-wing extremist Baruch Goldstein kills 29 Muslims on February 25 at a mosque in Hebron, Israel.

1995—12 people are killed when terrorists release deadly Sarin nerve gas in the Tokyo subway. Alfred P. Murrah Federal Building in Oklahoma City is destroyed by a truck bomb, killing 168 people.

1996—A truck bomb in Dhahran, Saudi Arabia, kills 19 U.S. soldiers at the Khobar Towers military barracks. Two people died as a result of a bomb explosion in Centennial Park during the Atlanta Olympic Games. In December, left-wing Tupac Amaru terrorists in Peru seize the Japanese embassy and hold it until the following April.

1997—Islamic terrorists kill 58 foreign tourists in Luxor, Egypt.

1998—Bombs at U.S. embassies in Kenya and Tanzania kill 257 people. A car bomb exploded by a breakaway IRA group destroys the center of Omagh, Northern Ireland, killing 29 people.

2000—The Al-Acksa Intifada begins. U.S.S. *Cole* is attacked in Aden Harbor by a small boat loaded with explosives.

2001—Islamic terrorists hijack four planes and use them to destroy the World Trade Center in New York City and damage the Pentagon in Washington, D.C.

Maps

The United States

Latin America

ATLANTIC OCEAN
PACIFIC OCEAN
Gulf of Mexico
Caribbean Sea
MEXICO
Mexico City
BELIZE
Belmopan
GUATEMALA
Guatemala
EL SALVADOR
San Salvador
HONDURAS
Tegucigalpa
NICARAGUA
Managua
COSTA RICA
San Jose
PANAMA
Panama
CUBA
Havana
HAITI
Port-au-Prince
DOMINICAN REPUBLIC
Santo Domingo
PUERTO RICO
San Juan
VENEZUELA
Caracas
GUYANA
Georgetown
SURINAME
Paramaribo
FRENCH GUIANA
COLOMBIA
Bogota
ECUADOR
Quito
PERU
Lima
BOLIVIA
La Paz
Sucre
BRAZIL
Brasilia
Rio de Janeiro
PARAGUAY
Asuncion
CHILE
Santiago
ARGENTINA
Buenos Aires
URUGUAY
Montevideo
N
0 500 Miles
0 500 Kilometers

Europe

Middle East and South Asia

Africa

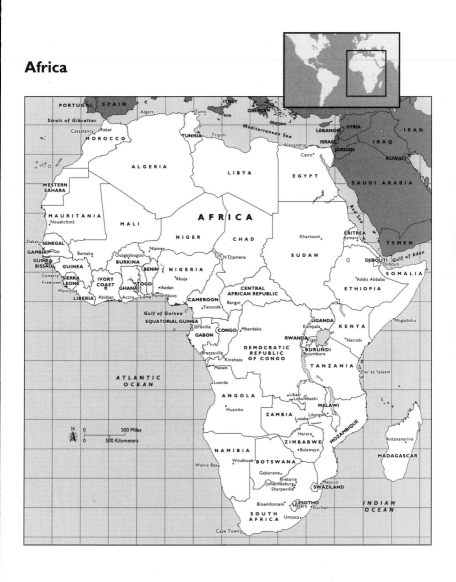

Texts

16 From "Six Dead After Church Bombing," *United Press International*, September 16, 1963. Reprinted with permission of United Press International.

18 From "An Israeli Airliner Hijacked to Algeria" from *The New York Times*, July 23, 1968. Copyright © 1968 by the New York Times Co. Reprinted by permission.

20 From "Belfast Bombings Kill At Least 1 and Wound 130" from *The New York Times*, July 22, 1972. Copyright © 1972 by the New York Times Co. Reprinted by permission.

22 From "A 23 Hour Drama" by David Binder from *The New York Times*, September 5, 1972. Copyright © 1972 by the New York Times Co. Reprinted by permission.

24 From "German Kidnapped; 4 Guards Are Slain" from *Reuters*, 9/5/77. Copyright Reuters Limited 1977. Reprinted by permission.

26 From "Ex-Premier is Discovered in Car on Downtown Street 54 Days After Abduction" by Henry Tanner from *The New York Times*, May 9, 1978. Copyright © 1978 by the New York Times Co. Reprinted by permission.

28 Excerpt from "Envoy Waite Detained by Hezbollah Forces, Diplomatic Sources Say" from *Los Angeles Times*, January 31, 1987. Reprinted by permission of the Los Angeles Times.

30 From "Town's Hall Used as Clinic, Then Morgue." Reprinted with permission of The Associated Press.

32 From "Gandhi is Murdered in Bombing" as appeared in the *Houston Chronicle*, May 22, 1991. Reprinted with permission of The Associated Press.

34 From "Blast rocks Trade Center" in *The Washington Times*, February 27, 1993. Reprinted with permission of The Associated Press.

36 From "Hundreds in Japan Hunt Gas Attackers" by Nicholas D. Kristof from *The New York Times*, March 21, 1995. Copyright © 1995 by the New York Times Co. Reprinted by permission.

38 From "Clues Are Lacking" by David Johnston from *The New York Times*, April 19, 1995. Copyright © 1995 by the New York Times Co. Reprinted by permission.

43 From "The Bombing of the World Trade Center in New York City" by Dave Williams as appeared in the *International Criminal Police Review*, No. 469-471, 1998. Reprinted by permission of the author.

49 Excerpts from "The Spider In The Web" as appeared in *The Economist UK*, September 22, 2001. © 2001 The Economist Newspaper Group Inc. Reprinted with permission. Further reproduction prohibited. www.economist.com.

59 "The Image" by Colson Whitehead. Copyright © 2001 Colson Whitehead. From *The New York Times Magazine*, September 23, 2001, Late Edition-Final, Section 6, Page 21, Column 1. Distributed by The New York Times Special Features. Reprinted by permission.

60 "The Weapon" by Stephen King as appeared in *The New York Times*, Sept 23, 2001. Reprinted by permission of the author.

61 "The Technology" by Jennifer Egan from *The New York Times*, Late Edition-Final, Section 6, Page 24, Col. 4, Sept 23, 2001. Copyright © 2001 by the New York Times Co. Reprinted by permission.

62 "Real War," formerly titled "The Thrill" by Judith Shulevitz as appeared in *The New York Times*, September 23, 2001, Section 6, page 28, Col. 4. Reprinted by permission of the author.

67 From "The Politics of Rage: Why Do They Hate Us?" by Fareed Zakaria, from *Newsweek*, October 15, 2001. Copyright © 2001 Newsweek, Inc. All rights reserved. Reprinted by permission.

103 "What is terrorism: the use of terror is more widespread and effective than is generally recognized." © 1996 The Economist Newspaper Group, Inc. Reprinted with permission. Further reproduction prohibited. www.economist.com.

112 From an interview with Brian Michael Jenkins, Deputy chairman of Rand Corporation by Paul Bagne from *Omni*, 11/1/94. Reprinted by permission of *Omni*, © 1994 Omni Publications International, Ltd.

118 "Terrorism in the Twenty First Century: Threats and Responses" by Yonah Alexander appeared in the June 1999 issue and is reprinted with permission from *The World & I*, a publication of The Washington Times Corporation © 1999.

128 "Both Sides Apply Term In Effort To Win People's Hearts, Minds Mideast Terrorism: War of Word" from *The Washington Times*, August 8, 2001. This article first appeared in *The Christian Science Monitor* on July 31, 2001 and is reproduced with permission. Copyright © 2001 The Christian Science Monitor. All rights reserved. Online at csmonitor.com.

136 "The Lone Gunmen" by Ehud Sprinzak, reproduced with permission from *Foreign Policy #127* (November/December 2001). Copyright 2001 by the Carnegie Endowment for International Peace.

141 "A Portrait of the Terrorist" by Jim Yardley, originally published in *The New York Times*, 10/10/01. Copyright © 2001 by the New York Times. Reprinted by permission.

159 "Shock Waves" by Jay Tolson et al from *U.S. News & World Report*, 9-24-2001. Copyright 2001 U.S. News & World Report, L.P. Reprinted with permission.

167 "Justice, Not War" by Kevin Danaher from *The Washington Post*, September 29, 2001, Edition: Final Section: Editorial. Reprinted by permission of Dr. Kevin Danaher, the co-founder of the San Francisco based human rights group, Global Exchange.

169 "Hama Rules" by Thomas L. Friedman as appeared in *The New York Times*, Editorial Desk: Section A, Foreign Affairs, September 21, 2001, p. 35, Col. 5. Copyright © 2001 by the New York Times Co. Reprinted by permission.

174 From "Media Terrorism" by Charles Krauthammer as appeared in *Harper's*, October, 1984. Reprinted by permission of the author.

177 "Caught by the camera; NBC's interview with a terrorist stirs up a controversy" by James Kelly from *Time*, May 19, 1986. Copyright © 1986 Time, Inc. Reprinted by permission.

181 "Rushing to bash outsiders" by Richard Lacayo from *Time*, May 1, 1995. Copyright © 1995 Time Inc. Reprinted by permission.

184 From "Terrorizing ourselves from now on, tighter security is the rule. But how much of our freedom will we sacrifice?" by Richard Lacayo from *Time*, September 24, 2001, Special Issue Publication. Copyright © 2001 Time Inc. Reprinted by permission.

192 "The Other War, Against Intolerance" by Richard Rothstein originally published in *The New York Times*, 9/26/01. Copyright © 2001 by the New York Times. Reprinted by permission.

194 "The Home Front, Letter to the Editor," as appeared *The New York Times*, Oct. 10, 2001. Reprinted by permission.

197 "Muslim Scholars Back Fight Against Terrorists" by Laurie Goodstein, originally published in *The New York Times*, 9/12/01. Copyright © 2001 by the New York Times Co. Reprinted by permission.

201 "Keeping Panic at Bay" by Jared Diamond from *The New York Times*, October 21, 2001. Copyright © 2001 by the New York Times Co. Reprinted by permission.

217 "Lessons in grief; a victim of terrorism brings what comfort she can to Oklahoma City" by Susan Schindehette and Don Sider/*People Weekly*, May 22, 1995. Copyright © 1995 Time Inc. All rights reserved.

221 Reprinted courtesy of *Sports Illustrated:* "Munich's Message" by Kenny Moore, SPORTS ILLUSTRATED, August 5, 1996, Copyright © 1996, Time Inc. All rights reserved.

228 "What Comes Next? Get back to normal? That place may be gone forever. America is heading, slowly, for someplace new . . ." by Nancy Gibbs from *Time*, Oct. 8, 2001. Copyright © 2001 Time Inc. Reprinted by permission.

231 Article by Jonathan Franzen as appeared in *The New Yorker*, September 24, 2001.

235 "Is terror the right response to terrorism?" by Larry Laudan as appeared in Vol. 79, *Consumers' Research Magazine*, 09-01-1996. Reprinted by permission of Consumers' Research Magazine.

239 "Aftershocks: Even as adults try to cope with fears touched off by the terrorists' attacks, they need to help their children heal" by Fannie Weinsten/*People Weekly*, Oct 8, 2001. Copyright © 2001 Time Inc. All rights reserved.

243 "Deciding What Our Loss Means" by Hans Butzer originally published in *The New York Times*, October 10, 2001. Reprinted by permission.

245 "Letter to the Editor, by Pearl Duncan, New York" dated Oct 10, 2001 from *The New York Times*, Oct . 11, 2001. Reprinted by permissions of the author.

245 "Letter to the Editor, by Seth Steinberg, New York" dated Oct. 10, 2001 as appeared in *The New York Times*, Oct 11, 2001. Reprinted by permission of the author.

Images:

cover, 94, 213 *bottom,* **254, 255** © AFP/Corbis.

16, 17 *top,* **18–19, 23** *bottom,* **24, 27** *bottom,* **27** *top,* **31** *top,* **34, 35** *bottom,* **155** *bottom,* **208, 210, 247, 252** © AP/Wide World Photos.

17 *bottom* © Danny Lyon/Magnum Photos.

19 *top,* **152–153** © David Rubinger/Corbis.

21 *bottom* © Central Press/Hulton/Archive by Getty Images.

21 *top* © Penny Tweedie/CORBIS.

22 © AFP Worldwide.

23 *top,* **209** *bottom* © Bettmann/Corbis.

25 *top,* **25** *bottom,* **28** © Keystone/Hulton/Archive by Getty Images.

26 © Hulton/Archive by Getty Images.

29 © Al Jawad/SIPA Press.

30–31 © Letkey/AFP Worldwide.

209 *top* © TimePix.

211 © Reuters/TimePix.

212–213 © Munoz/SIPA Press.

248 © Kelvin Boyes/Getty Images News Services.

249 *bottom* © Burton McNeely/TimePix.

249 *top* © Vittoriano Rastelli/Corbis.

250 *top* © EPA-European Press Agency/PA Photos.

250 *bottom* © Rawass/Sipa Press.

251 © Parekh, Swapan/Black Star.

253 © Getty Images News Services.

Every effort has been made to secure complete rights and permissions for each selection presented herein. Updated acknowledgements, if needed, will appear in subsequent printings.

Index